# GARDEN STYLE
# SOURCE BOOK

# GARDEN STYLE
# SOURCE BOOK

## Design Themes for
## Every Type of Garden

*ANDREW WILSON*
All pictures supplied by the
**GARDEN PICTURE LIBRARY**

HEADLINE

*For Barbara and in memory of Ray Maskery*

A QUARTO BOOK

Copyright © 1989 Quarto Publishing plc
First published in Great Britain in 1989 by
HEADLINE BOOK PUBLISHING PLC

HEADLINE BOOK PUBLISHING PLC
Headline House
79 Great Titchfield Street
London W1P 7FN

**British Library Cataloguing in Publication Data**
The Garden style source book.
1. Gardens. Landscape design
712'.6

ISBN 0-7472-0171-4

This book was designed and produced by
Quarto Publishing plc
The Old Brewery
6 Blundell Street
London N7 9BH

Project Editor Susan Berry
Senior Editor Kate Kirby

Designer Hugh Schermuly
Illustrator Vana Haggerty
Planting Diagrams David Kemp
Horticultural Consultant Peter Thurman

Editorial Director Carolyn King
Art Director Moira Clinch
Assistant Art Director Chloë Alexander

Typeset by Ampersand Typesetters, Bournemouth.
Manufactured in Hong Kong by Regent Publishing Services Ltd
Printed by South Sea Int'l Press Ltd Hong Kong

Special thanks to Steven Wooster

# CONTENTS

# ~ INTRODUCTION ~

The Oxford English Dictionary describes the garden as a piece of ground devoted to growing flowers and fruit. This could be interpreted in a number of different ways but, no matter how we approach it, for many of us owning and cultivating a portion of this earth is both precious and important.

Growing up as I did in the conurbation of South Lancashire quickly revealed that ownership of a garden was something to be valued and that it was a definite status symbol. I used to cycle out to small woodlands or copses filled with spring bluebells and, sitting by my bicycle, would imagine living in enchanted seclusion.

Those early fantasies were important to me, but it was not until I studied landscape architecture that I came to appreciate the true complexity of fulfilling my daydreams. I also gained an understanding of the possibilities. The styles of garden or landscape design are myriad and the possible combinations of hard and soft elements were an exciting revelation to me. Some years on, having learned a great deal about garden design, I still feel myself to be on the periphery of some enormous source of knowledge, as if standing on the shore and looking out to sea.

Planting design is far more than just using pretty flowers, glorious autumn tints, seasonal effects or fashionable new hybrids. It includes these elements, but in a context that is much wider and more appropriate to the garden in question. Equally, hard landscape design is not simply a facility for the display of objects, and it is quite definitely not about dotting baroque cupids, ivy-clad rustic birdbaths or gnome-like concrete horrors around the garden. These pedestrian absurdities abound and I am not sure why. So how should you decide which elements of planting or decoration deserve a place in your garden?

Taking the plant material first, plants are three-dimensional objects: they have shape and form, and occupy a space. They can be grouped together in delightful associations to form a structural mass. This framework of plant material can enclose, shelter, screen and channel views. It can also provide a backdrop, like scenery on a stage, against which more colourful, interesting or architectural material can be displayed.

Simple ground-cover planting may provide a carpet of foliage. Hedging can be used as a dense wall of evergreen material or as a transparent deciduous screen of green-leaved lacework. Shrubs or trees can be used for less formal structure, and give shape and strength to borders or planting areas.

Into these niches, specimen material may be arranged either as single plants or as a sculptural association of various plants, perhaps sharing some common characteristic or attribute, such as sword-shaped leaves or contrasting light and dark foliage.

*The seclusion offered by a terrace is for many the ultimate achievement in garden design. The textured surfaces of foliage and paving form a room, defining space in a way which is both versatile and informal. The atmosphere is evocative of long summer days and warm sultry nights when outdoor living comes into its own.*

**Left** *The combination of hard and soft materials is successfully emphasized here by strong colour. The earthy tints of terracotta and gravel are complemented by the inspired combination of* Delphinium, Hemerocallis, Hosta *and* Kniphofia.

**Below** *The textures of hard materials such as timber, loose-laid cobbles and concrete are important in this architectural association with fine grasses and water.*

**Left** *High contrast and chiaroscuro play a part in this design where filtered sunshine reflects from glossy leaves and warms the timber decking. Beneath, the dark, damp shade and the coolness of water are lost in dramatic planting.*

**Right** *The strong architectural shapes and bold textures of tropical foliage are successfully massed as a setting for sculpture. The rich, varied leaf forms contrast their relaxing greens with the smooth, geometric paving in warm terracotta tones. The design is simple but well co-ordinated and therefore very effective.*

Equally, colour schemes may be applied to individual associations or, if scale permits, across several areas of planting. Architectural groups may incorporate dynamic spikes, spreading palmate shapes and strongly veined leaves. Seasonal attributes can be combined so that individual plants lend some character to the group when others do not.

The permutations are endless, given the variety of plants to choose from. The important elements are that the plants relate to each other and their spatial arrangement. The specimens or specimen groups should be visible from many different angles. Allow space around the planting groups to set them apart from the general mass within borders based on simple geometry. An appreciation of shapes and forms should follow as distance, light, shade and perspective excite the eye. In larger spaces be bold with colour and texture, massing plants together in simple groups with specimen plants for punctuation. Balance the attributes of plant material and simplify plans rather than elaborate on them.

The same principles should apply to the design of hard elements, such as paving, fencing, pergolas and walls. Simplify combinations of materials and use them honestly: each element has some attribute which should be recognized. Concrete is not, and never will be, stone, but it can still be an exciting medium to use. Discover the potential of different hard materials in combination with planting, and eschew imitations and fake ornamentation in particular.

The juxtaposition of the asymmetric, organic forms of nature against symmetric man-made structures is often exciting and worthwhile. Soft landscaping disguises and frames hard materials which, in their turn, balance the random filigree patterns of planting. Together they should be used as a palette of materials, colours and textures, combined together to produce a variety of styles and to create a space for living.

The aim of this book is to provide some guidance as to how to create or adapt your garden space. Whichever style you opt for, the keynotes should be simplicity, balance, unity and geometry. Adhering to these ideals makes the possibility of creating a garden that is beautiful, fulfilling and satisfying a reality.

# THE
# FOLIAGE GARDEN

Colour in planting design is most frequently associated with flowers – their brilliant hues and delicate shapes are seen as the epitome of beauty and grace. Although it would be difficult to ignore their charm, it pays to look beyond the transient flashes of inspiration. Foliage, particularly evergreen foliage, creates a permanent feature in the garden but often attractive colour is revealed in deciduous species in the darkest months of winter. Herbaceous plants show dramatic growth over short periods of time, expressed chiefly in foliage bursting fresh from the earth.

Foliage does more, then, than simply enhance the flowers it frames. It enriches the garden with architectural shapes and forms, interesting colour variations and a variety of textures.

## FOLIAGE FORMS

Foliage is found in so many guises as to make generalization difficult. It is easiest to consider foliage in terms first of screening or background scenery and then in terms of specific accent or specimen planting.

In the former category is a vast number of species with inconspicuous or neutral leaves, which can be used to screen or to create privacy. They also provide structure or a background wash of colour or texture against which more flamboyant material is displayed to dramatic effect. Control and understatement form the essence of good design in this respect for, as with flowers, too much decoration, colour or pattern simply confuses. The great herbaceous borders of the traditional English garden were all framed by the smooth dark velvet-green of yew hedging.

In the other category, accent plants demand attention. These are the jewels of foliage planting whose qualities and characteristics are dynamic, bold and theatrical. The grass-like texture of bamboo *(Miscanthus* or *Arundinaria),* the sword-shaped leaves of New Zealand flax *(Phormium tenax),* the glossy heart-shaped spread of the fatsia leaf *(Fatsia japonica)* and the gigantic veined and fleshy splendour of *Gunnera manicata* indicate the variety and range of plant material available. The art of using these plants well lies in the careful positioning of specimen plants against a neutral backdrop.

Alternatively, foliage plants can be massed together in stands of the same species. Where space permits create patterns and textures in bold swathes

*The qualities of decorative foliage are often expressed in waterside planting, where large leaves and spiky rushes seem to embody the concept of water itself. Here the overhanging canopy filters and dissipates the sunlight, producing strong patterns and a multitude of shapes and colours.*

but in small gardens, combine a number of individual plants with differing leaf characteristics in small informal groups. Foliage can contrast in terms of shape, texture and colour or associations of plants may be developed which share a common characteristic, such as leaf colour. The same association, if successful, could be repeated throughout a garden (depending on its size) to introduce a feeling of continuity and rhythm. In effect you are sculpting with plant material, working in three dimensions with foliage, light and space.

## SEASONAL ATTRIBUTES

The seasons affect plant associations. The changes are unavoidable and challenging, but also most welcome. Spring brings fresh new growth and a sense of excitement and anticipation, changing and maturing the planting design. Summer develops the foliage, and the bright sunshine plays light against shadow. Luxuriant growth revels in warmth and deep, cool greens in the garden relax the mind, especially in association with water.

The more golden light and deeper shade of autumn complement new colours in the dying foliage. Gardeners are often tempted to clear and tidy their gardens too quickly at this time but the lingering coppers and golds of strewn leaves provide the last links with summer and dead foliage has a sweetness of its own.

As autumn turns to winter, the foliage recedes and the framework of the plant itself is introduced. Here the texture of bark or the colour of stems become the focal points in planting design, complemented by the tracery of the branches. Fiery crimsons of dogwood *(Cornus)*, delicate purples of

willows *(Salix)* and papery layers of birch *(Betula)* or maple *(Acer)* bark are some of the options available to the designer. The cinnamon trunk of the strawberry tree *(Arbutus unedo)* or the fabulous tracery of the Indian bean tree *(Catalpa bignonioides)* are elements often forgotten in garden design. Remnants of berries or rose hips echo the rich colours of winter and seem particularly bright and attractive against stark branches.

Evergreen plant material provides continuity through these seasons and also complements the naked branches of deciduous plants. It is important to think across the full spectrum of evergreen material. Although conifers, so widely used, have much to offer in form and texture broad-leaved evergreens provide a valuable alternative. The evergreen or holly oak *(Quercus ilex)* is dark and majestic, ivy *(Hedera)* climbs or covers the ground in a multitude of varieties and cabbage palms *(Cordyline australis)* offer an exotic quality.

The blue-grey leaves of the *Eucalyptus* characterize an unusual evergreen species which can be grown as a shrub or tree depending on the species, and are valuable in theme planting where foliage colour is as important as flower. The magical quality of white or silver plant associations is so over-used as to be almost a designer cliché but the frosted, mystical charm of such planting is difficult to ignore. Alternatively fiery combinations of reds, purples and yellows provide drama and excitement.

Playing with coloured foliage, as with texture and shape, is rather like trying to find the correct sequence for a combination lock by trial and error. Many combinations are possible and every so often you succeed in cracking the code. The effect can be inspirational, but lasting beauty and a sense of balance are usually achieved through control and restraint in choosing plant material and simplicity and caution in arranging shapes and forms.

*Far left* The feathery textures of Acer palmatum *and* Dryopteris filix-mas *work successfully together. Their delicate shapes catch the sunlight, and the decorative shadows and contorted tracery produce intricate patterns of light and shade.*

*Left* The rigid geometry of topiary relies on the fine textures of box (Buxus sempervirens) *for edging and yew* (Taxus baccata) *for the main structure. Contained within are themed borders of foliage or flower colour which contrast well with the dark dense hedging.*

*Adjacent left* The curving path becomes lost in a deep border of foliage colour and contrast with climbers, conifers and ground-cover clothing almost every surface. The fallen tree leads the way alongside the path, decorated with Hedera helix *and* Viola × wittrockiana.*

## BETH CHATTO'S GARDENS, COLCHESTER, ENGLAND

Beth Chatto uses foliage plants as most other people do flowers – mixing colour, texture and form. Her associations rely on co-ordinated or blended ranges of colour or contrasting bold patterns against fine textures. *Hosta, Iris, Rodgersia* and a wide range of ornamental grasses fill the borders.

The garden is full of interesting combinations of plants which often rely on unusual species. (Beth Chatto's nursery specializes in the production of species and varieties less commonly seen in the garden.) Colour is restricted to broad sweeps where possible, to allow the perennial foliage plants to decorate, while trees or shrubs give structure, shade and scale. The bold forms of *Gunnera, Rodgersia,* and *Rheum* are juxtaposed with *Alchemilla, Miscanthus,* or *Hosta* while *Hedera, Rubus, Geranium* or *Astilbe* carpet the ground. Her aim of filling borders or beds with plants works to spectacular effect – bare soil is rarely visible.

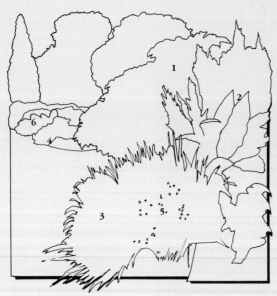

**SCHEME FOR A FOLIAGE GARDEN**

1 *Gunnera manicata*
2 *Rumex hydrolapathum*
3 *Iris pseudacorus*
4 *Alchemilla mollis*
5 *Myosotis palustris*
6 A mixture of *Lythrum salicaria, Astilbe, Veronica, Hosta* and *Mimulus*

*Right* The waterside associations balance the rich patterns and textures of foliage against the bright colour of flowers. Reflections are sharp and decorative in the mirrored surface of the still, dark pool. The water seems to disappear beneath the powerful leaves of Gunnera manicata, *as if into some submarine cave below.*

**Above** *The massing of foliage in this corner relies on the dramatic qualities of* Hosta *for effect. The rich blue-green of* Hosta sieboldiana *catches the eye, emphasized by the yellow-green backdrop and surround. The planting rises in stages from a formal lawn edge – from low ground-cover to tall dark trees against which the more interesting plant material can be set off.*

**Left** *The use of bold green foliage as ground-cover in this shady area is rich and decorative. The patterns of light and shade and the mixing of matt and reflective leaf surfaces are an important feature. Flowers are few and far between, relegated to summer borders where light will emphasize their colour.*

# EXOTIC FOLIAGE

The term "exotic" is difficult to apply to plants as it simply means "introduced from abroad", although it is generally used to refer to plants from warmer or tropical regions. Their foliage is often remarkable or unusual in some way and the textures and patterns produced by these species are dramatic and exciting. They are often seen massed together in imitation of some jungle scene and, although their qualities can be seen in this rather jumbled style, the most appropriate way of using these plants is in splendid isolation, where their architectural style can be best appreciated. The fabulous palm leaves, graceful and elegant with their Venetian-blind-like shadow stripes, the curving banana leaves with dramatic flowers and fruits hiding beneath, and the incredible size and structure of the giant water lily *(Victoria amazonica)* are just a few examples of exotics which never fail to impress. Use exotics in pots for specimen effect or for decorating terraces or walks. In the right climate, they can be planted into formal avenues.

**Left** *The strong contrasts of light and shade that are such a feature of tropical climates suit the dramatic shapes of these exotics. Shining spears of polished greenery flash in the dark undergrowth and a stone figure sits pensively beneath the glossy foliage of* Ficus benjamina.

**Above** *The form of these palm trees lends an elegant air to the formal avenue. Their tall, slender trunks, pillar-like, are free of foliage. Above them, there is an explosion of green fans of arching leaves of the current season's growth.* Trachycarpus excelsus *and, in some cases,* Chamaerops humilis *are appropriate fan plants for use in formal situations such as this.*

## FOLIAGE PLANTS FOR DRAMATIC EFFECT

Exotic foliage plants rely chiefly on size for their effect. Use the giant split leaves of *Musa* for their bright green arches and decoration. Palms such as *Chaemerops humilis* and *Trachycarpus fortunei* produce fan-shaped leaves. *Phoenix dactylifera* and *P. canariensis* produce elegant arches of finely divided leaves. *Cordyline australis* produces architectural spikes on top of slender trunks. For architectural specimens closer to the ground try *Agave americana* or *A. victoriae-reginae*. *Yucca gloriosa* or *Y. filamentosa* have less rigid leaves. Use the creeping fig *(Ficus pumila)* for fine ground coverage or as a climber for bare walls. Other species of fig, such as *F. benjamina*, will make tall specimens of shiny green foliage. Use the delicate leaves of *Acacia* for light shade (but beware the vicious thorns). *Eucalyptus* is a less aggressive choice, with pale blue-grey foliage that shimmers in the light.

**Left** *The simple architecture and decking allow the foliage to dominate this garden – the timber decking with regular slats contrasts well with the decorative arching leaves of* Musa. *Palm leaves and the broad foliage of* Strelitzia reginae *add interest to the low ground-cover as specimen plants. Flowers are few and far between, and pots provide the principal ornamental emphasis.*

# WALKWAYS AND PATHS

The soft tactile qualities of foliage combine with the harder textures of paving material in pathways through the garden. Use the two materials to sculpt routes or walks as if through virgin territory. The jungle-like foliage of herbaceous plants can encroach upon the paving edge or more formal lawns and clipped hedging to give scale and grandeur to gracious avenues. Pleaching leaves light and space for more decorative foliage or paving patterns beneath whilst the trimmed hedging stands above head-height, creating a formal enclosure. Pergolas have a similar effect with more rampant and uncontrolled growth, but they also introduce direction and rhythm. Their rigid geometry can be counterbalanced by training stems and leafy garlands. It is a good idea to use foliage to create secrecy and screening, and to obscure the destination of pathways, thus inviting curiosity and a spirit of discovery. Any element of surprise or seclusion is always welcome in a garden.

*Below left These heavy timber cross-beams, along with the stone paving beneath, have aged to a weathered grey. The rampant growth of the Russian vine* (Polygonum baldschuanicum) *is colonizing the stone with its greedy tendrils and red-brown stems, the mid-green foliage hanging in trusses. This climber can grow over 5m (16ft) in a single season and can withstand severe pruning. It must be used with care, sparingly, as it will easily suffocate other species. Nevertheless, the decorative leaves and misty green flowers of Alchemilla* mollis *thrive beneath its mantle.*

*Below The pleached Fagus sylvatica encloses space but allows the pathway beneath to continue uninterrupted. Forest bark has been used to give the pathway a softer, less formal appearance, fitting well with the meandering line and informal planting that densely carpets the ground. The yellow flowers of Buphthalmum* salicifolia *and Verbascum are echoed in the yellow-greens of foliage beyond: the effect is warm and sun-filled.*

**PLANTS FOR FOLIAGE EFFECT**

In identifying foliage plants for bordering pathways, consider their eventual height before choosing or purchasing.

For canopy interest choose trees such as *Catalpa bignonioides*, *Paulownia tomentosa* or *Liriodendron tulipifera*.

Hedging plants can grow tall depending on the adopted maintenance regime. Use *Fagus sylvatica* or *Carpinus betulus* for deciduous effect or *Taxus baccata, Ilex aquifolium* or *Buxus sempervirens* for evergreen foliage.

*Wisteria sinensis, Parthenocissus henryana* or *Vitis coignetiae* have interesting or colourful foliage for use with pergolas.

Ground-cover plants such as *Alchemilla mollis, Rubus tricolor, Hedera colchica, Hosta sieboldiana* and *Bergenia stracheyi* "Silberlicht" have a range of foliage shapes and sizes, and look good interplanted with architectural or decorative species.

*Symphoricarpos* × *chenaultii* "Hancock" has delicate fern-like foliage which contrasts superbly with *Hedera helix* "Hibernica".

*Left* The stone-paved walk is just identifiable as a route through luxuriant foliage. The densely packed leaves of Hosta crispula *and* H. elata *are juxtaposed with* Iris pseudacorus. *The contrast between the large fleshy veined leaves of* Hosta *and a sword-shaped leaf such as* Iris *is an important design element. The image can be used over and over again as a source of rich texture. The pathway is almost incidental here, the foliage dominating all, encroaching on the paving. The leaves are dense enough to inhibit any weed or interfering growth, leading to lower maintenance. No soil is visible here, only a lush carpet of patterned greenery.*

# THE FOLIAGE FRAMEWORK

Foliage can be used as a structural material either in a formal sense or more informally as a frame or backdrop to give a feeling of enclosure or shape to planting. It is also frequently used alongside hard surfaces either as a direct contrast in texture or in order to creep and tumble across paving or over walls to soften their rectilinear shapes. For a more formal effect, low hedging of *Buxus sempervirens* will finish or edge a border against pathways in order to frame the planting within or to neaten the boundary. The evergreen conifer *Taxus baccata* is the common hedging material against which more decorative planting can be displayed. It also creates structure and restricts views.

In less formal situations foliage plants can be used for texture, colour and form in their own right. The effects of light and shade resulting from texture generate decorative patterns which are difficult to match in other materials. Neutral shades or tones offset more dramatic flowers or foliage or an ornamental surface of ground-cover may frame statuary in a sea of shining leaves. Climbing plants may be used with trellis-work to obtain a hedge-like structure. No trimming would be necessary and the plants can be left to ramp away. It is possible to achieve more dramatic effects using larger-leaved species of climbers such as *Wisteria* that have pinnate leaves and a feathery texture.

*Below In a formal garden the shining grey-white of statuary is offset well by the rich green of* Taxus baccata. *The silvery-white leaves of* Lamium *add interest against the texture of forest bark.*

*Left The clipped hedges of* Cypress *and* Buxus *ensure precise containment and shape in the formal garden. Within this rigid framework, the more spontaneous growth of* Philadelphus *and* Rosa *can be restrained and controlled.*

**Left** *This unusual use of* Hosta sieboldiana *takes advantage of the plant's rich leaf colour and texture. If left alone in the right situation this plant grows to enormous proportions and here the figure is becoming swamped, saved only by the delicate frame of* Wisteria sinensis *"Alba" behind.*

**Above** *This vertical screen and archway is covered with the large leaves of* Hedera colchica *which can reach up to 20cm (8in) across. Such dense growth not only obliterates unsightly features but provides a strongly textured surface.*

# ARCHITECTURAL FOLIAGE

The term "architectural foliage" describes species with particularly bold, decorative, prominent or striking leaf form. These plants are often used as individual specimens or in groups to introduce strong texture, dynamic shape and theatrical exuberance in a border or planting area. Spiky sword-shaped leaves are common in this category, together with large palmate, crenulated or feathery patterns. Leaf-veining, striations and textures are used to decorative, reflective effect. High gloss surfaces are often contrasted with hairy or down-covered leaves or hand-shaped palm leaves with large flat shapes. The use of texture, shape and form in this way is an essential part of contemporary garden design. These abstract qualities are particularly appropriate with modern architecture, where spartan surfaces and restrained minimalism need powerful planting statements. Wide areas of garden may be planted with simple, textural ground-cover planting from which these architectural shapes explode with power and energy. Groups of contrasting foliage plants bring dramatic interest whilst massed groups of the same species look strong and exciting. Flowers are less important and play a secondary role to leaf form, unless highly structured and complementary. Colour should not be too vivid or it will distract from this style.

*Below The leaves of* Hosta *are beautifully and dramatically veined, showing their main design characteristic. The leaves reach 30cm (12in) wide and individual clumps increase over time to reach sizable proportions. Variegated-leaved plants are available but the plain-leaved forms look much more elegant.*

*Left This tropical terrace area is planted with a whole range of bold foliage material. The enormous leaf of the banana plant (*Musa*) predominates, fanning out above the large clumps of* Strelitzia reginae. *The simple geometry of the surrounding architecture and the regular strips of timber decking allow the dramatic foliage shapes to dominate the garden. Palms and ground-cover fill the spaces between the specimens' finer textures. The* Strelitzia *bears its exotic bird-of-paradise flower to provide additional colour and interest.*

### PLANTS FOR DECORATIVE EFFECT

The essence of architectural foliage plants lies in their theatricality. The large leaves of *Gunnera manicata, Fatsia japonica, Petasites, Hosta* and *Rodgersia* contrast well with the dynamic spikes of *Phormium tenax, Yucca* and *Cordyline australis.* On the smaller scale, *Iris, Festuca, Helictotrichon* and *Miscanthus* are equally dramatic and the fine leaves of *Arundinaria* combined with the segmented stems are tall and graceful. More decorative foliage may be found in the silver-leaved *Eryngium* and *Onopordum* or in darker *Euphorbia, Mahonia, Rheum* or *Acanthus.* *Juniperus* × *chinensis* "Pfitzerana" or *Viburnum plicatum* "Mariesii" have less dramatic foliage but the arrangement of leaves along the stems is particularly architectural. Trees such as *Acer, Catalpa bignoniodes* and *Paulownia* have bold, decorative foliage and shrubs such as *Hamamelis, Magnolia* and *Garrya elliptica* are also useful. Use climbing plants to carry foliage high against structures or into less decorative tree canopies. *Wisteria, Tropaeolum* and *Vitis* are all to be recommended.

**Left** *The gigantic leaves of* Gunnera manicata *dominate this waterside planting area, reaching up to 1.8m (6ft) wide. The plant also generates huge cone-shaped structures reaching approximately 1m (3ft) high. For a herbaceous perennial, that represents an incredible growth rate. The leaves are heavily textured and incised, creating strong shadows that increase the dramatic effect. The foliage is contrasted with the sizable leaves of marginal planting. Against the fine texture of the lawn, these foliage plants announce the presence of water, identifying its meandering path. Luxuriant plants grow well in the damp moist soils associated with water and the leaves achieve their greatest size under these conditions.*

# GROUND-COVER

Ground-cover planting is functional as well as decorative. By carpeting the ground with dense planting, maintenance requirements are reduced, as weed growth is eliminated by competition. In this way, a lawn is simply another form of ground-cover which uses fine grasses, closely mown to produce a textured, hopefully weed-free, surface. Vigorous foliage plants such as *Hedera, Rubus,* and *Gaultheria* produce a flat carpet of leaf as an alternative. Taller-growing species, such as *Hosta, Lavandula* and *Hypericum,* will cover the ground equally well if planted densely enough and larger shrubs may also be used, though often a lower carpet of cover is needed as well. Specimen shrubs may be planted in clumps or groups into low ground-cover which then becomes a neutral backdrop of textured greenery. The reduction in garden maintenance is a necessity for people who lead busy lives and ground-cover planting goes some way towards achieving this goal. Using a lawn as ground-cover, however, is the exception to this rule, as it is a major drain on resources, in terms of time, labour and expenditure.

**Above** *This dramatic arrangement relies on the strength and power inherent in the Japanese statue and in the fern, erupting upwards and outwards from the border. A variety of ferns lend themselves to ground-cover use as although their spread is wide and dense, their texture is light and feathery. The grass here is left relatively long and is open to invasion from field and meadow plants, which many would think of as weeds. This is simply an alternative to the manicured lawn rather than incorrect procedure.*

**Left** *In deep shade, ground-covering foliage plants are probably the only solution. In this wooded dell, ferns have been allowed to cover one side of the bank while ivies (Hedera) and vinca jostle together on the opposite side. In very deep shade ivy is one of the few plants that will survive.*

## USEFUL PLANTS

Ground-cover plants are used for their characteristically dense foliage, which effectively blankets the ground and suppresses weed growth. Low shrubs and herbaceous material also fall into this broad category if, by dense planting, they can achieve an overall cover of the ground. The spread of each plant and the planting width are important in ensuring the ground is adequately covered. Usually planting distances of 30-45cm (12-18in) are recommended although smaller spreading species may be 15cm (6in) apart. Suitable plants for low flat cover include *Hedera, Rubus tricolor, Juniperus horizontalis, Stachys* and *Cotoneaster dammeri*. Hummock-forming species may also be used such as *Armeria, Festuca glauca* and *Alchemilla*. Plants which form a higher carpet of foliage are *Hosta, Epimedium, Geranium, Hypericum* and *Genista*. Grass-like species such as *Luzula, Iris, Crocosmia* and *Kniphofia* are useful for vertical emphasis and fine texture. If taller-growing shrubs are used, consider planting below with shade-loving species such as *Hedera, Gaultheria, Hosta* or *Cornus canadensis.*

*Left The interlocking pattern is strengthened by the imaginative use of colour in ground-covering foliage and gravel paving. The silver-grey of Santolina is particularly strong and scented. The dark purple of Berberis contrasts well in leaf form and colour while the blue-green of Teucrium unifies the scheme. Often these intricate patterns and knots need maintenance to restrict plants to the desired size and shape. More decorative ground-cover plants may be incorporated into the spaces between the hedges to produce flower or further foliage interest. Otherwise decorative gravels in a variety of colours can be used to strengthen or identify the pattern. The whole of the surface is then covered in some way to prevent weed growth and to maintain the intended design, which needs only occasional clipping to keep its contours.*

# SCREENING AND SHELTERS

As an alternative to structural walls of brick, stone or concrete, a screen of foliage has much to offer. The effect of light percolating through trellis, covered in green foliage, is rich in pattern and *chiaroscuro*. The sharp contrast of light and shade falling on foliage against decorative and plain walling is equally effective. Climbing plants are an excellent device for blurring the hard angles or strong geometry of man-made forms.

Hedging can also achieve similar results. Dense compact growth is possible using well-maintained box *(Buxus sempervirens)* or yew *(Taxus baccata)* as evergreen screens. The colour of these dense hedges often reads from a distance as black or the darkest of green-browns. As a much lighter less impenetrable screen use deciduous material such as hornbeam *(Carpinus betulus)*, hawthorn *(Crataegus monogyna)* or for autumn effects, beech *(Fagus sylvatica)*, or oak *(Quercus robur)* which keep copper-coloured foliage throughout the winter as long as they are pruned. These more open screens, as with climber-covered trellis, allow views through to the other side, intimations of something beyond. Besides the rich greens and yellows of foliage, they borrow life, sound and colour from the world beyond the one they contain.

**Right** *The strong red colour of the outdoor furniture add drama to this terrace, which feels like a clearing in woodland. No flower colour is included in the structural planting which manages to enclose the terrace with texture, form and dappled shade. The effect is rich and mellow, giving the illusion of space and deflecting attention from the boundaries of the site.*

**Above** *The structural form of this trellis is similar to architectural detail in screening or creating enclosure. Space is restricted within a framework but the light from areas beyond infiltrates the screen.*

**Left** *The random patterns of the stone wall are picked out in light and shade as a rich enclosure to the delicate greens of fern and maple. The romantic gothic archway beckons to a dark woodland on the other side, as if it were the entrance to some secret underworld.*

# THE WATER GARDEN

Why is water so fascinating? Perhaps very simply because it is the original *aqua vita,* the very water of life. Whatever the reason, there is no doubting that water holds a certain influence over us all. It cleanses, refreshes, quenches our thirst, cools us, relaxes us and provides the key to life itself, as it feeds and nourishes luxuriant plant growth.

### THE USE OF WATER

Water has been in favour for thousands of years as an element in garden design, in Ancient Egypt, South America and Japan. It was used to soothe and cool, to irrigate or decorate. In Japan the water was skilfully manipulated to mirror the landscape, either with large still pools or with rushing waterfalls. In Europe a more formal style developed and water often became the focal point in a design, channelled and retained into geometric symmetry.

Water adds vitality to any garden. A still pool will introduce new dimensions of colour, reflection, light and shadow. As the wind disturbs the surface, the patterns change or blur.

Movement in a water feature produces sound which can vary from a murmuring trickle to a thunderous cascade. Fountains can be ornate and sculptural, with water as an incidental element. Powerful jets or sprays can thrust the water high into the air or dissipate it into tiny iridescent droplets. Bubble fountains disturb the surface of a pool or gurgle and erupt with splashes and ripples.

### POOL SHAPES

The water feature itself may provide a flat sheet of water to reflect light or surrounding plant material. A deep dark pool will provide the best reflections. The pool does not need to be large and the illusion of depth can be created by painting the inner walls of the pool black, using a black butyl liner or by using dark shingles or pebbles on the pool floor. The true depth of the water is thus difficult to gauge and light is reflected purely from the water surface.

Alternatively, a shallow feature can be used to display the qualities of the pool floor. Mosaic may be used, decorative tiles or simple gravels and

*This canal feature illustrates the particular charm that water can express in a garden setting. The honey tones of evening light are captured on the water's surface. Only the fine tracery of pondweed emerges from below, dispelling the illusion of a dream world beyond.*

pebbles give texture. Ripples and waves on the surface deflect the light and break up the pattern.

A formal pool is usually defined by its edge and designed to a rectilinear or geometric shape which forces the water into an obviously man-made pattern. Here the canals, rills and pools of the large estates or stately homes can be imitated on a smaller scale. In contrast, informality is achieved by breaking or interrupting this rigid formal geometry either by creating softer, meandering lines and more amoebic shapes or by introducing plant material. Even so, an underlying, simple geometry and proportion must still underpin these designs.

Although these pools may still be man-made, their character is gained from emulating nature. Those which are most successful have no easily defined edge. The water may lap against a shingle beach or the pool edge may be lost in boulders or marginal plant associations such as reed or iris beds.

These water features can be rich in wild life as birds, waterfowl and insects are all drawn to the water as a rich feeding habitat. Plant associations are varied and luxuriant, from delicate water lilies and bladderworts on the water surface to towering spikes of reed mace or expansive gunnera at the pool's margins.

## CHANGE OF LEVEL

Introducing changes of level into a water feature enhances its appeal. Movement from one pool to another results in waterfalls through giant boulders or rock strata or, in a cascade, over the smooth lip of a pool edge, or even in a trickle through a bamboo pipe.

The water feature itself can become a moving fountain or spout with no still or standing water in evidence. Jets which gush through pebbles or gravel can simply drain back through the porous surface to be collected below, recycled and pumped up again.

## POOL CONSTRUCTION

More formal pools can be constructed in concrete, perhaps with a decorative facing of ceramic tiles. Surrounds of stone or brick can be applied to make a more attractive surface. Many hard materials may be used as cladding as long as the water is retained by concrete or prefabricated pool liners, often in fibreglass or butyl.

The more informal pools are traditionally formed in puddled clay although butyl lining material is now a much more flexible option. The main aim is to prevent seepage of water into porous rock or surrounding soil and sub-soil. Natural pools will only form where the parent rock below is impervious or where the soil is heavy clay.

The hard edge of the more formal pool is difficult to disguise and these designs lend themselves to incorporation into paved areas and terraces. The more flexible butyl-lined or puddled-clay pool can easily be hidden by overhanging vegetation or more informal paving such as loose gravel, pebbles and boulders. Timber decking can overhang the edge of the pool so that the water disappears beneath the paving.

## PLANT MATERIAL

Various plant associations can be incorporated in or around the water feature. The pool itself can play host to aquatic plants, some of which are hidden beneath the surface. These are often the essential oxygenating plants such as curled pondweed *(Potamogeton crispus)* and water violet *(Hottonia palustris)*, which keep the water fresh.

Of the floating-leaved plants the most prized is the exotic water lily *(Nymphaea)*. Various forms and colours are available which enjoy different water depths. They can be vigorous growers and may shade the pool, which upsets the balance of the habitat. If planted in baskets in PVC or wire their spread is easily controlled. The baskets are submerged and rest on the bottom of the pool or they can be supported on blocks to vary the depth of planting. Frogbit *(Hydrocharis morsus-ranae)*, water chestnut *(Trapa natans)* and bladderwort *(Utricularia vulgaris)* provide alternative species.

Marginal plant material is probably the richest source of foliage form in association with water. The sword shapes of iris, bulrush, arrowhead and reedmace can be contrasted with the giant textured leaves of *Gunnera, Hosta, Rheum* and *Rodgersia*. More interesting for their flowers are the skunk cabbage *(Lysichiton americanus)*, arum lily *(Zantedeschia aethiopica)*, *Cardiocrinum* and marsh marigold *(Caltha palustris)*.

Adjacent to the water, plants that enjoy moisture or which can provide interesting reflections should be massed together for colour and texture of skilfully placed as specimens. Astilbes, day lilies, knotweed and primulas provide flowering displays, hart's tongue and royal ferns, or sedges and

grasses provide texture.

Specimen plants can punctuate the water's edge – bamboo, Japanese maple *(Acer palmatum)* or New Zealand flax *(Phormium tenax)* for example. If space allows, trees such as alder, birch, willow and swamp cypress can accentuate the vertical scale to contrast with the horizontal emphasis of the body of water. Care should be taken with the siting of deciduous species as leaf drop in autumn can choke the pool.

## SWIMMING POOLS AND JACUZZIS

Water features provide excitement and fun. Swimming pools can be integrated into the overall design of the garden though safety usually demands a more formal treatment of banks or pool sides. They can be surrounded, at least in part, by plant material offering a screen or shelter. The pool lining need not be aquamarine or turquoise as so often seen, which often looks out of context with more subdued planting or paving.

For smaller gardens hot tubs or splash pools can provide as much fun as a swimming pool. They can even be accommodated alongside small terraces, relatively close to the house. Most water features will lend themselves to lighting to provide an interesting focal point when the garden is used in the evenings, or simply to enable the pool to be enjoyed from the house.

**Far left** *Water need not dominate a garden but can be almost incidental, complementing a border or association of plants. This simple container provides a shallow pool of rainwater and allows the colourful spikes of* Astilbe *and* Ligularia *to decorate with their feathery plumes and tall rockets.*

**Above left** *The gentle curve of the pond, disguised by luxuriant planting, is accentuated by the brick surround. This forms a more formal edge and also allows the lawn to be trimmed easily. Such a visible coping must be precisely laid in order to contrast successfully with the more informal planting. An alternative approach would be to introduce a verge of wild plants and longer grass between the lawn and the water, making a hard edge unnecessary.*

**Above** *This formal feature relies on light paving and dark water for contrast. The stepping stones are directional and focus the eye on the structure beyond. More mature planting would help to hide the pool edges whilst adding to the atmosphere of a woodland clearing.*

## LONGSTOCK PARK, STOCKBRIDGE, ENGLAND

The gardens of Longstock Park play host to a wide variety of aquatic and bog plant associations. Many are suitable for much smaller-scale gardens and do not rely on space for their effect. Use the bold foliage plant material even in restricted areas and contrast it with spikes and feathery flowerheads. Larger expanses of water need bold planting for balance. Use broad swathes of smaller marginal planting such as *Caltha palustris* or *Primula* and punctuate them with the spreading elegance and drama of *Rodgersia* or *Gunnera*. Fine grasses or sedges produce striped reflections and delicately offset the larger leaves of *Hosta*. A backdrop of trees such as *Salix* or *Alnus* gives light feathery reflections. Choose from larger-leaved species to give deeper shade and contrasting scenery. The light filtering through breaks the heavy shade and the dappled effect introduces movement and depth to the waterside. Ferns or bracken echo the woodland character and rejoice in the damp pungent atmosphere.

**Above** *This simple crossing point, formed from timber beams, is tucked into waterside planting almost as an afterthought. The textured ground-cover of* Campanula carpatica *nestles alongside with clear purple-blue flowers, contrasted with the much more architectural foliage of* Zantedeschia aethiopica.

**Right** *The decorative qualities of marginal or bank planting are an important contrast to the glassy stillness of the water surface. Reflections produce intricate patterns and the colourful primulas add splashes of warm colour.*

## SCHEME FOR A WATER GARDEN

1 *Iris laevigata*
2 *Polystichum setiferum* (form)
3 Vinca minor
4 Candelabra primulas
5 *Hosta sieboldiana*
6 *Lysichiton*
7 *Gunnera manicata*
8 *Primula florindae*

**Above** *The brilliant yellow of monkey musk* (Mimulus luteus) *brightens the waterside planting with splashes of vibrant colour. The yellow patches have a sunshine warmth compared with the cool clear water beyond.*

**Left** *This quiet stream meanders through dense bankside planting under the cool shade of woodland. The plants are richly textured with the feathery plumes of* Aruncus dioicus *towering above the water.* Aponogeton distachyos *spreads its dark glossy leaves across the surface.*

# CLASSICAL WATER

Classical water features rely on formal, usually symmetrical arrangements with the water itself retained by hard edges, which emphasize the strong shape. The pools are rarely planted except for serene water lilies, fine rushes or reeds. Essentially the water surface is plain and uninterrupted to provide a flat reflective surface beneath which Koi carp feed, their metallic flashes providing the only decoration.

Fountains are used to introduce movement, often in fine jets or sprays, sometimes pouring from a deity or the mouth of a gargoyle frozen in stone while concentric ripples break the surface of the water creating crazy patterns of light.

Hard paving such as stone, brick or concrete slats, may overhang the edge or low walls can retain the water at a higher level. These features are imposed on the landscape in sophisticated shapes, totally created by man, yet somehow beautiful and immaculate. Unlimited space suits these graceful creations but in small gardens simplicity and pure geometry will be more successful in creating the desired effect.

**Above** *Lichen-covered stone slabs frame this simple pool. The changes of level are restrained and introduce visual interest with pediments for free-standing pots. The fountain disturbs the water surface with quiet ripples, creating gentle murmurs of watery noise.*

**Left** *This pool relates well to the scale of the formal avenue, and acts as a dramatic focal point. The lines of the clipped hedge are mirrored in the shape of the pool, which, typical of formal features, is edged with large stone slabs. The fine spray of the fountain creates a splash pattern on the surface, complementing the texture of the floating lily pads, but more defiant use of moving water would have worked equally well in this instance.*

### POOL SHAPES

Formal shapes in water gardens should be pure and geometrically obvious. This gives them strength and simplicity, and leaves the water itself to provide the focus of attention with its movement, reflections and sound. Hard edges, retaining walls or paving are left clear of clutter, furniture and planting in order to identify and accentuate the shape, which should relate and be sympathetic to the surrounding garden. The hard edges or raised walls should be of stone, cast slabs or rendered brickwork. They are best situated in gravel or grass, so that simplicity dominates both in the lines and the planting. The shapes are often either squares or circles, which provide a stability and elegance. Elongated shapes such as rectangles, ovoid forms or triangles create a movement through the axes, along which the eye tends to travel. These shapes are well employed in a linear garden or where there is another focal point, a building or statue for example, beyond the pool. Combinations of these shapes can be used for more complex effects. The pool itself should remain unplanted except possibly for a few round-leaved plants, such as waterlilies, or linear ones such as thin-leaved irises or rushes, which retain the simplicity of the design. If the purpose of the pool is as a home for plants then it is an idea to opt for an informal design.

**Left** *The water lilies erupt from this yawning feature set into hard surfaces. The small pool is endowed with drama by the treatment of the retaining wall forming the backdrop. The arch is theatrical, the stone directional and the climbing plants add romance and decoration. The water itself is almost invisible, choked with glossy leaves, making the true depth of the pool difficult to gauge. The dark waters suggest a deep well plunging into the earth below.*

# FOUNTAINS

Fountains allow water to become dynamic and exciting. Depending on the force or power of the water pump, they can transform still, reflective pools into a mass of white foam, or shoot droplets of water high into the air, sparkling with captured light as they fall, pulling rainbow arcs out of thin air. They can murmur or chatter, boiling just above or below the surface. They can drip or slide across a surface, splashing into deep pools below and polishing hard materials to a glistening sheen – bubble fountains disturb the surface of the pool without throwing water into the air.

Fountains are essentially about water itself, which should be the focus of attention. Highly decorated or sculptured pump or water pipe mouthpieces can break up the water as it hits the air, helping it to splash down in complicated moving patterns across figures, rock outcrops or terraces. Fine perforations allow the water to spring outwards in delicate sprays and spouts, or it may be thrown against a surface to explode again in intricate tracery.

Water movement results in sound, an important element in fountain design. The sound level should be definite, either a forceful roar, a loud splash or a gentle murmur. A half-hearted trickle or light patter will probably annoy and irritate, as it ceases to become purely background noise. The fountain head itself should be in keeping with its surroundings or with the prevailing architecture, although stunning effects can be achieved with contrasts of old and new styles and materials, or with formal against informal.

Scale is also important. If space is restricted, then consider a single jet or spout. Decorative gargoyles may be fixed to a wall behind a pool to cover the source of water (though these are now so commonly used as to be something of a designer cliché). Hide or decorate the source with foliage, use pots or vases to pour water into the pool or use free-standing sculpted heads or busts. Often a bold feature in a tight corner will create the illusion of space: tiny spouts or jets can be overlooked or insignificant.

On a larger scale, use a multitude of fine jets to create architectural shapes in the air or use bold foamy white water rocketing skywards before thundering down to earth. Shallow pools of water brimming over a terrace or shallow bowl are much more restrained and must be accurately constructed to allow water movement around the complete circumference. The water may fall in cool thin sheets or drip decoratively onto the next layer. The water may run into a catching pool or simply onto the paved surround or plinth to drain back for recycling. The latter effect allows us to get close to the moving water, to encounter its physical properties and to enjoy its sounds close at hand.

*Below This slender sculpted figure dances or runs whilst catching a cascade of clear water. The water drains to the ground and into the circular pool which lies below. The pump will usually be hidden in a sunken chamber, often disguised by plant material, and the piping will run through the base and up through the sculpture to erupt mysteriously high in the air. The sculpture itself could be further simplified by recessing the plinth or losing it altogether. The figure standing on the granite set base would then appear to belong to the pool.*

**Left** *The large bowl of this solid fountain catches the spray before spilling water into the lily pond below. It is difficult to combine moving, disturbed water with aquatic planting which usually enjoys quiet still pools. By catching the water and restricting its effect this fountain and bowl work well. The weight appears to be supported by the water itself which is decorated with lily pads and flowers. A similar effect could be obtained by using a bubble fountain in the main bowl instead of the extra tier and fine spray. Water could then be allowed to curtain the pedestal with sheets of clear water.*

**Above** *The adoption of marine-associated figures or symbols is quite common in fountain design. Choose large or bold elements with strong simple decoration or form. This large, exuberant fish positively explodes with life, though caught as a frozen sculpture. Again the plinth plays an important and obvious role in this fountain. Rather than simply supporting a sculptural work, the base becomes an integral part of the whole design.*

# REFLECTING POOLS

The reflective potential of water is one of its most attractive and exciting qualities. A still, dark pool will produce a mirrored surface shining with light and colour, replicating images from the surrounding landscape. Gentle wind-blown ripples break the images into waving patterns of movement and water lilies float on the peaceful luminous liquid. Reflective pools should be simply shaped and large enough to accommodate an adequate length of reflected image.

How you place the artefacts or planting is also important and depends on both the position of the viewer and the objects to be reflected in the surface of the pool. These objects should be treated as specimens or focal points to draw the eye. They should be framed by or contrasted with neutral or dark foliage. Reflected sky will introduce light against which foreground objects can be counteracted.

Elements can be placed into the water to increase their apparent size or to create optical illusions where the surface of the water is difficult to identify. Bold shapes and strong leaf forms reflect well and spiky or sword-shaped leaves can provide excellent contrast with the flat circular leaves of water lilies or the textured architecture of marginal plants such as the large-leaved *Gunnera* and *Rheum*.

**Far left** In relation to the formal pool, the Ben Nicholson sculpture is dramatically placed, allowing the reverse image seemingly to float beneath. The dark foliage and the shadow behind contrast starkly with the white sculpture; the tints of autumn provide a softening kiss of gold to decorate the quiet mirror of the pool. The sky is almost eliminated from this view, letting much darker tones predominate and allowing the sculpted surface to shine out.

**Left** The combination of strong reflections against a clear luminous sky is magical and the autumn colours or branched tracery provide additional decorative interest. Water features of this scale can take full advantage of changing light effects and dramatic sky scapes. The lake can accommodate the full length of reflected specimen trees, and the surrounding landscape of woodland and green meadows ties the whole scene together with solidity and strength. The simplicity of the bank treatment and the general massing of shrubs and trees is important to the overall effect. Specimen plants punctuate the landscape, displaying their particular character, shape or colour, enhanced by the quietness of the scene.

**Above** The dark grey pebbles on the pool bed help to define the reflections against a contrasting tone. A decorative random pattern is also introduced which creates exciting visual play with the surface reflections and light, together with the floating lily pads. The pebbles are also functional as they can be used to disguise or cover the roots of the water lilies. The contrast between reflected sky and reflected artefacts is particularly strong.

# SMALL FEATURES

Water is an element in garden design which can be made to work on any scale. Its versatility lends a particular charm to small features which can occupy very little space. A bubble fountain or spout caught perhaps in a pot or trough or simply splashing onto pebbles or gravel below produces attractive sound. Ferns, mosses and textural ground-cover plants soften the dampness around the feature, catching the eye with sparkling water splashes. A cool relaxing corner is complete with sensual messages of flickering light, escaping splashes and bubbling resonance. Avoid an ostentatious display around the feature and opt instead for decoration that is simple and restrained. In fact, a single decorative element will provide a more powerful effect than busy patterns and a clutter of ornament. Handsome foliage is difficult to match for elegance or beauty and looks sublime in association with water.

**Left** *An old stone trough is used as a focal point to hold water. The bold foliage of an ornamental gourd is allowed to decorate the white-washed brickwork breaking the monotonous surface and drooping down into the water. The curious tap with its snail motif forming a bracket is both decorative and amusing.*

**Far left** *A circus clown bursts through a hoop to squirt water into a circular pool. The metallic sheen of the sculpted form echoes the foliage colour and contrasts with the organic grain of the timber edge. The mechanics of the fountain are hidden in the undergrowth behind.*

**Above** *This feature is simplicity itself, adding interest and reflective pattern to a purely functional element. The pebbles could perhaps have been used more successfully to hide the rim of the container which would then be buried beneath. Any simple watertight container could be used in this way to reduce cost.*

**Right** *A fascinating small grotto has been created in the narrow space between two town houses. The raised pool and surrounding arch have been created in York stone, clad with various attractive ivies. Otherwise colour has been sensibly limited to white climbing roses and to the pelargoniums in pots.*

# CROSSING WATER

Part of the pleasure of including a sizable water feature in a garden is to be found in crossing the water. This is usually done by a bridge or by stepping stones, which can be more fun. Crossing points are normally included for pleasure as, from a functional point of view, bridges can cause problems. With garden machinery, stepping stones are definitely out of the question. The great temptation with bridges and stones is to think of them in miniature, merely as decoration. However they do attract use, and it is important that they should be stable, strong and in proportion to the garden space or water feature.

Crossings should appear as the only obvious way of passing over the water; if not they become redundant. Hide more circuitous routes around the pool with heavy planting and emphasize the route to the stones or bridge. Handrails are not essential and if used with low timber decking often spoil the simple effect of a jetty stretched just above water level. Generally the form of the bridge depends its usage, height above water level and width. If the bridge is going to be used as a viewing platform then a handrail is certainly required, to allow people to lean over the edge in relative safety. Rails and supports should be strong but not cumbersome; bridges should appear light and elegant, as if hanging in mid-air.

*Right* The elegant arch of this timber bridge flies over a richly planted stream. The handrails are formed of thick rope suspended from fine steel uprights to give a delicate, draped appearance which is nevertheless still functional. Rope can often be used to support climbing plant material but in this case there is sufficient softness in the marginal planting to merit a more architectural style. The bridge provides an obvious crossing point, offering a means of sampling the delights in store on the opposite bank.

*Left* Sawn timber sections of varying size provide stepping stones here, more for decoration than function. Timber and water work well together and the plant material softens and brightens the effect but timber can eventually rot and in damp shade will become slippery. The timber rounds would thus need replacing from time to time.

## ORGANIZING STEPPING STONES

Stepping stones issue an open invitation for us to enjoy water at close quarters – to step into the middle of a pool or stream and enjoy a fresh perspective. They can be decorative or purely functional but, whichever the case, people will still want to use them. Their stability is essential and their foundations must be adequate to ensure their permanence and to prevent rocking. The individual stones must not feel or appear precarious and you need a generous size to allow you to stand upright without feeling the need to balance. A relatively smooth but non-slip surface is also essential and the gap between individual stones should appear possible as an easy step rather than as a jump. Introducing a meandering or slightly random pattern to the arrangement of stones makes for a more interesting effect. In larger features, a larger stone or group of slabs can form an island or meeting point in the centre of a path.

If the stepping stones continue the line of a path on either side of the water without apparent interruption then many people will cross without any qualms as it seems the natural road to take. This is even more so if the approach paths also consist of stepping stones, embedded in the grass or earth. On the other hand stepping stones, particularly irregularly shaped ones, at an angle that breaks the line, engender a feeling of adventure and slight daring when the water is crossed, possibly as it gives the impression of a strong current pushing the stones aside.

# MARGINAL PLANTING

The margins of a water feature allow you to plant a host of interesting species which enjoy water and boggy conditions to grow alongside plants known more for their decorative qualities. These groups of plants may not enjoy the same growing conditions and certainly the whole concept of many garden water features relies on introducing and artificially containing water in what would otherwise be a free-draining site. Emergent plants can easily be accommodated by planting into earth mounds in the shallower waters of the pool, above the waterproof membrane.

Similarly, plants used as specimens for decorative reflections can be easily introduced around the pool. Those species that are truly marginal and enjoy bog conditions, such as *Caltha, Glyceria* and *Iris,* must be planted into an artificial bog. By extending the waterproof membrane below ground level beyond the proposed water's edge, you retain the water within the soil to produce just the right conditions in which the plants will flourish. The liner is buried out of sight and the damp-loving plants thrive alongside those found in drier soils, allowing a wide variety of plant associations to succeed.

## SELECTING MARGINAL PLANTS

Few areas within the garden are as replete with luxurious architectural or decorative planting as the marginal borders around still or running water. For sheer drama, the enormous leaves of *Gunnera manicata, Rheum* or *Petasites* cannot be surpassed. These plants thrive in rich, moist soil that merges with the water's edge. They look particularly good when grouped with bold clumps of smaller-leaved plants which enjoy a similar position, such as *Hosta, Rodgersia, Ligularia* and *Filipendula.* Spiky-leaved plants usually enjoy the very water's edge with their roots in the boggy margins or even in the water itself. Plants such as the bulrushes, *Typha* and the irises contrast well with the vast rounded leaves on the banks behind them. The yellow-flowered *Trollius* and *Caltha,* kingcups, form small clumps along the water's edge together with the bright whorls of the candelabra primulas. The water forget-me-not *(Myosotis palustris)* weaves its way through the other plants, adding speckles of pale blue. One of the large plants to enjoy the mud edges is *Lysichiton Americanus,* the bog arum or skunk cabbage, with its curious yellow arum-like flowers in spring followed by huge lettuce leaves in the summer. Colour is provided by the purple loostrife, *Lythrum salicifolia,* which throws up spires of bright purple flowers in late summer and into autumn. Contrasting well with this, liking a similar position, is the flowering rush, *Butomus umbellatus,* with spiky leaves and airy domes of pink flowers.

*Far left The bold foliage of* Ligularia *punctuates the much finer dissected foliage arranged around the pool. The stems and leaves are tinged with bronze, complementing the flowers.*

*Left The edges of the pool are difficult to identify as the emergent plants mix with the ground-covering* Cotoneaster. *The delicate textures of* Alchemilla mollis *will always associate successfully with marginal planting.*

# ELEGANT AQUATICS

The term "aquatic" relates specifically to those species that grow in several inches of water, unlike marginal plants which may survive with their roots in water but which normally flourish in boggy conditions. The water lily (*Nymphaea*) is the best known aquatic, its floating leaves adding texture to the water's surface, punctuated with elegant, formal, waxen flowers. Water lilies are extremely vigorous in still pools, so be careful they do not choke the water and stifle other species. To prevent this plant them in wire baskets, which will restrict their growth. Grow *Aponogeton distachyos* or *Stratiotes aloides* as alternatives and incorporate oxygenating plants such as *Lagarosiphon major* or *Ceratophyllum demersum*. Allow areas of clear water around or between the planting to provide balance and some reflective quality to the water. Large expanses of water look best with great stretches of lily pads.

**Left** *The stillness of this pool allows* Nymphaea *to colonize, with its cool sculptural flower-heads and shiny round leaves. The plants do not like to be disturbed and would not prove successful in moving water. Their texture and colour work well here against the dark water. Behind, the graceful heads of* Cyperus *bend down, almost as if drinking, on slender stems.*

**Above** Nymphaea *"James Brydon" rests its blood-red flowers on a mat of wet foliage. The plant needs a 90cm- (3ft-) depth of water and a rich loam for good rooting and growth. The leaf edges often crinkle and reflect the light in delicate patterns, complementing the still waters beneath. A wide variety of flower colours is now available – including white, strong crimson, burgundy reds and glowing yellows.*

**Above** *The deep purple-blue of* Iris *is made more vivid and powerful by the brilliant spots of yellow. The colour combination is most successful seen against the flat leaves of* Nymphaea, *and texturally the leaf forms contrast well. This combination of marginal and aquatic planting is well worth experimenting with as a rich source of interest.*

**Right** *The famous water lilies of Giverny appear as textured islands of foliage and colourful flower in the mirrored pool surface. The elegant arch of the bridge in subdued green produces subtle shadows and reflections while the marginal planting serves to emphasize the glass-like water, full of light and dancing colour.*

# THE ALL-SEASONS GARDEN

One of the most satisfying elements in gardening is the experience of seasonal change – a soap opera acting out birth, growth, productivity and untimely death played annually outside the window. The changing phases are expressed with an incredible beauty all too often taken for granted. By choosing plant material carefully, the seasonal indicators can be manipulated to produce a much more lasting effect in our gardens.

## SPRING

Spring is synonymous with birth, or rebirth. Tangible symbols of that renewal are most evident in the plant material around us as it responds to rising temperatures. Daffodils *(Narcissus)*, forsythia *(Forsythia × inter-media* "Lynwood"), grape hyacinth *(Muscari)* and hyacinth *(Hyacinthus orientalis)* push their flower heads through the cold earth in search of light. Yellow, lemon and blue flowers introduce long-awaited colour into the garden, and release delicate perfumes.

Although these colours are each welcome, there is always a danger of producing unfortunate colour-clashing combinations. Stronger flower colour belongs to the heat of summer and in the frail spring light vivid tulips, dense pink cherry blossom and the strong yellow of forsythia look gaudy and harsh and do nothing for each other. White blossom, lemon yellows and pastel blues make a far more sympathetic colour scheme.

Large areas of colour or groups of plant material can be used to prevent individual flowers becoming lost or insignificant. Naturalized planting of bulbs is often the most successful way to treat them, usually achieved by scattering bulbs randomly and then planting them where they fall.

Blossom is a major element in the landscape in late spring with the delicate pinks of almond *(Prunus dulcis)*, crab apple *(Malus sylvestris)*, the whites and creams of hawthorn *(Crataegus × monogyna)* and spirea and the stronger sherbet-pink of the Japanese cherries *(Prunus)*. The shape of the latter is often rather artificial due to their method of propagation and they can look structured and forced against the free exuberance of

*In the soft golden light of autumn the yellows, russets and browns of flowers and dying foliage are bathed in complementary light. Here the tall spikes of* Kniphofia *are almost burnt out in the last flash of orange-yellow .*

indigenous species. These are best used as single specimens against a dark background to allow full appreciation of their effect. The flowers are short-lived but the petals make a handsome carpet on the ground.

## SUMMER

By June and July the pale green of new leaf has darkened and flower colour becomes the dramatic focus. Colour and scent are synonymous with summer flowers and the drone of nectar-seeking insects completes the picture of heat haze, warmth and relaxation. Magical white schemes, hot and sultry reds and oranges, rich and elegant gold and yellow combinations or dark purples and magentas can all be expressed in flower. Few other mediums possess their strength and purity of colour.

Foliage, too, is essential and plentiful in summer – a white garden would look washed out without a dark evergreen backdrop to provide a frame and a contrast. The reds and oranges need bold foliage and spiky leaves to complete their burning image. Yellow and gold foliage appears permanently sun-kissed and purples and blue greens echo the dark cool shades in the blue border. Deep dramatic shadows from foliage create depth in a planting scheme and contrast strongly with the burning sunlight.

Flowers as decorative elements need not be restricted to the traditional chocolate box charm of the rose. Intricate patterns are uniquely organized in the passion flower *(Passiflora caerulea)*, sweet scent drips from the long racemes of wisteria *(Wisteria sinensis)* which can ramble over pergolas or up into trees. Giants of flower such as larkspur *(Delphinium)*, foxglove *(Digitalis purpurea)*, bear's breeches *(Acanthus mollis)* and foxtail lily *(Eremurus robustus)* tower over tiny forget-me-nots *(Myosotis sylvatica)* or gypsophylla *(Gypsophylla paniculata)*.

Use decorative annuals as infill ground-cover plants. The tradition of planting them in rows or formal patterns creates a mosaic from the plants, points of colour with little relation to each other. Grouped together the colour is much stronger and the plants grow close to reduce maintenance.

Herbaceous species are at their full height in summer, often with huge leaves filling the spaces in the border. Paeonies decorate with layered flowers in early summer followed by the rocket spires of larkspur *(Delphinium)*, red hot poker *(Kniphofia)* and lupins *(Lupinus)*.

## AUTUMN

Early mists and sparkling dews herald the arrival of colder temperatures and signal the end of the season for deciduous and herbaceous material. The maidenhair or fossil tree *(Ginkgo biloba)* is a deciduous conifer which

*Left* With spring comes a great flush of life into the garden, most evident is the tree blossom of Prunus, Malus, Crataegus, and Pyrus. *Their delicate pink and white blooms are best matched below their canopy with the paler lemon-whites of* Narcissus *"Cantatrice" or* N. *"Cheerfulness". Leave the more vivid reds and yellows of* Tulipa *for bold individual displays.*

*Right* The frosts of winter can easily damage more tender species but the beauty of evergreen material is often emphasized by the sparkling white crystals. Juniperus × media *"Pfitzerana" is an elegant shrub in any season but its layered structure and slightly drooping branches are accentuated here in their frozen beauty.*

drops golden fern-shaped leaves upon the ground. Larch *(Larix decidua)* drops fine needles of copper.

As the flowers of summer fade their fruiting bodies remain, often forgotten as an autumnal feature. Rose hips sparkle long into winter, their shiny red spheres catching the light. Particularly vivid are those of *Rosa moyesii.* Horse chestnuts and sweet chestnuts drop to the ground to reveal their polished fruits. Berries cover rowans *(Sorbus aucuparia),* hawthorns *(Crataegus monogyna),* guelder rose *(Viburnum opulus)* and elder *(Sambucus nigra)* with splashes of red and claret colours.

Climbing plants can produce spectacular displays which transform house walls or a pergola in autumn. Virginia creeper *(Parthenocissus quinque-folia)* or Boston ivy *(P. tricuspidata)* rival any maple for vibrant autumn red and the golden hop *(Humulus lupulus* "Aureus"*)* complements with soft yellow. *Clematis tangutica* bears yellow lantern-shaped flowers followed by silky seed-heads, imitating Chinese lanterns *(Physalis alkekengii)* in the border below. The rich burgundy of vine *(Vitis coignetiae)* is spectacular with leaves up to 30cm (1ft) across, which can be used with the delicate abutilon *(Abutilon megapotamicum)* flowers carried well into autumn.

## WINTER

In winter the garden is all too easily dismissed. Flower interest is sparse and delicate but should be planned more carefully for that. Foliage is often relegated to evergreens battling bravely through freezing temperatures, but deciduous species frequently have more to offer. The leafless plants rely on other qualities to attract attention. The Westonbirt dogwood *(Cornus alba* "Sibirica"*)* shines through the gloom with brilliant coral red stems, the violet willow *(Salix daphnoides)* has much softer purple shoots covered in white bloom. Ornamental bramble *(Rubus cockburnianus)* and roses such as *Rosa rubrifolia* or *R. rugosa* have coloured or bristling stems.

The tracery of branches decorates the landscape. The stunted horns of sumac *(Rhus typhina)* left after a blaze of autumn colour are strong against the delicacy of silver birch *(Betula pendula)* with its metallic white trunk. Paperbark maple *(Acer griseum)* with its cinnamon layers of bark offers much more to the winter garden than insignificant dwarf conifers so beloved of garden centres and nurseries. Perhaps the most beautiful and graceful of the species with winter interest is the autumn cherry *(Prunus subhirtella* "Autumnalis"*)* whose tiny pearl-like flowers are suspended on delicate dark branches, framed against the ice-blue winter sky.

Down at ground level the pale cream flowers of Christmas rose *(Helleborus niger)* see out the cold temperatures. The stronger mauves of cyclamen *(Cyclamen coum)* produce a more prominent display and the scented flowers of Chinese witch-hazel *(Hamamelis mollis)* and mahonia *(Mahonia japonica)* float exotic perfumes through the frosted air.

## AN ALL-SEASONS GARDEN, HOOFDDORP, NEAR AMSTERDAM

In the gardens at Hoofddorp, near Amsterdam, individual plants are massed together with differing seasonal qualities so that no single area is devoid of interest for any great part of the year. Such groupings are essential in any garden if you are to appreciate the complete cycle of plant growth – a single mahonia with its golden winter flowers or a solitary pyracantha with decorative berries can look lost, go unnoticed or be out of keeping with neighbouring plants at the particular time of year.

Trees may succeed as single specimens as their dominant size and shape, particularly in small gardens, can provide the garden theme. Thus the strong colour of an *Acer* in autumn can easily set the tone or character of a garden or border for that time of year. Perhaps the easiest season to deal with is summer when annual plants can be introduced to create splashes of a particular colour to complement the permanent planting of the garden. Containers could be filled with white alyssum, blue lobelia and sizzling red or pink pelargoniums. They can stand alone or could be fitted neatly into empty spaces or dull corners to excellent effect.

*Right The summer colours enliven the low, ground-hugging planting. Had the foreground container been larger it would have filled the paved area with more abundant colour and related better to the dominant grasses.*

*Far right The dying foliage of* Iris *and* Salix *droops in an array of gold and green above a mirrored, watery surface. The colours are stunning, yet tinged with sadness, heralding the onset of winter. Enjoy these rich hues and contemplate the decorative qualities of the dying plants.*

*Above The red-tinged foliage of* Mahonia japonica *is covered in dew before or after a winter frost. This is a true all-seasons plant, flowering with lemon-yellow blooms from autumn to spring, its strong perfume filling the surrounding air. It has the bonus of handsome evergreen leaves and bluish-black berries.*

*Left The vivid tones of* Lysimachia punctata *are echoed in the ground-covering version,* L. nummularia. *Their summer colour is bold and full of sunshine yellow. Seen against the cool reflective water and the bright green marginal planting, this strength of colour is most successful.*

*SCHEME FOR AN ALL-SEASONS GARDEN*

*1 Miscanthus floridulus*
*2 Salvia nemorosa* "Superba"
*3 Nepeta × faassenii*
*4 Pelargonium × hortorum*
*5 Foeniculum vulgare*
*6 Lysimachia punctata*
*7 Butomus umbellatus* (flowering rush)

*8 Ligularia dentata*
*9 Chrysanthemum padulosum*
*10 Tagetes erecta* (African marigold)
*11 Mesembryanthemum* bellidiflorum
*12 Liastris spicata*
*13 Veronica spicata*
*14 Lysimachia punctata*

# THE GARDEN IN SPRING

As new growth emerges all around with fresh green foliage or bursting flower buds, the excitement of spring is unmistakable. The promise of warmer days is mingled with the realization that the rigours of winter are gone. Often the flowers of spring are obvious before the leaves; pink or white blossom on thin black branches can be framed dramatically against the sky. As silver-grey buds open, brilliant emerald splashes emerge to fill the empty canopies of deciduous trees and shrubs. Bright yellow daffodils *(Narcissus)* in broad sweeps toss their heads and shimmer in the wind of open woodland or meadow while in the sheltered forest, bluebells *(Endymion)* unfurl their ethereal amethyst-blue bells. In later spring the rhododendrons and azaleas have pride of place with incredible displays of colour in their intricately structured flowers. Used carefully in association with other shrubs and trees, they can be brilliant and majestic, but in pure stands they can be overpowering in flower, and dull or lifeless afterwards in leaf. It is better to use species that have interest and character at other times in the year rather than those whose glories are over in a few short weeks.

*Below* *The elegant oval heads of certain tulips* (Tulipa) *open into spectacular cup-shaped flowers. This* Tulipa *hybrid bears soft lemon-yellow cups outlined against the more dramatic stems of crown imperials* (Fritillaria imperialis), *which will flower later in the season.*

*Left* *This electric combination of pinks presents a stunning and unusual use of colour. The pale clear pink of* Prunus *is supported in mid-air by ebony tracery above the shocking magenta of* Azalea. *The density of the flower mass helps to create the strength of colour and allows a balance between the two groups. Unfortunately, this can only be a short-lived effect lasting for a month at the most. After flowering the foliage of both plants is neither interesting nor noteworthy.*

## SUCCESSIONAL EFFECTS

Rather than concentrating on a particular seasonal effect, group plants together with different characters for different times in the calendar. Alternatively, use species with secondary characteristics that may be of benefit or importance at some other time. *Prunus sargentii* or *Crataegus phaenopyrum* produce blossom in the spring and vivid leaf colour in the autumn. *Amelanchier* also follows this pattern and other forms of *Crataegus* are prolific berry producers. *Hamamelis mollis* produces fragrant spidery flowers early in the year and the large velvet leaves are richly coloured in autumn. *Mahonia's* lemon-yellow flower racemes are followed by blue berries and *Iris foetidissima* has decorative seed pods which follow purple flowers. The heads split open to show the scarlet seeds within. Various roses are followed after colourful flowering by spectacular hips in shiny red, black or purple, and the wide decorative flower panicles of *Sorbus* or *Sambucus* turn into glowing heads of berries, offering a rich harvest of autumn colour.

*Left* *The strong blue of bluebells* (Endymion non-scriptus) *is softened by mingling with the fresh green of the woodland grass. Eventually, as the woodland canopy fills with leaf, the ground will become densely shaded and the flowers will fade to green seed-heads. The* Rhododendron *and* Azalea *beyond will also change to dark green foliage and the overall view will be quite different. For the spring, however, the effect is magical.*

# THE GARDEN IN SUMMER

Summer is the season that garden lovers yearn for and enjoy most. Foliage and flowers fill borders and containers with rich colour, enhanced by bright sunshine or soaked by thundery showers. Strong scents and perfumes prevail long into the evenings and the garden can be enjoyed as a true outdoor room, an extension of living space. The brightness of annuals brings incredible masses of flower colour which can appear from early summer through to late summer or early autumn. Tobacco plants *(Nicotiana)* are particularly long-lasting, with masses of flowers from white to deep imperial purple, all sweetly scented. Petunias decorate with their colourful trumpets in a wide variety of pinks and lavender purples, matched only by the papery petals of sweet peas *(Lathyrus odoratus)*. Perennials such as *Delphinium, Agapanthus* and lupins *(Lupinus)* suit flowering borders as single specimens or, better still, in substantial specimen groups.

Plant any annuals between perennials and shrubs to strengthen or consolidate colour schemes or to carpet the ground beneath larger plants in solid colour. Alternatively, fill pots and containers with densely planted annuals to produce overflowing displays, dripping with flowers.

*Below Where space is restricted, annual planting can provide a rich and colourful display. Containers must be watered well and regularly if you want to ensure a luxuriant display. Here* Pelargonium, Tropaeolum *and* Petunia *are used for vibrant colour against the stark walls and paving.*

*Left The colour co-ordinated heads of* Petunia × hybrida *flow along the border, forming a colourful edge to both lawn and pathway. They clash with the strong green-yellow of* Euonymus *however, which does not rest easily with their lively colour mixes. The relationship between permanent shrubs and annuals should always be carefully considered before planting.*

**Below** *The escaping flowers display an exuberance seen only in summer months when the climate favours uncontrollable growth and free flowering. Spilling onto the steps,* Geranium, Lysimachia, Hedera *and* Cerastium *show a wild side to their character.*

**Left** *Restraint in the use of summer annuals has paid off in this scheme where dark velvet petunias and* Impatiens *have been planted in bold clumps of colour. The more restrained pink-lilac of* Geranium *echoes the delicate pink of* Rosa *beyond. This subdued use of colour produces a unity which is pleasant and satisfying, and which preserves the character of the garden.*

# AUTUMN COLOUR

The vivid colours of autumn foliage need as much control as flowers in their use in garden design. The strength of colour is difficult to judge as most plant material is supplied or planted over the dormant months of winter after the leaves have fallen. Species such as *Quercus, Acer* and *Liquidambar* have brilliantly coloured foliage in autumn in fiery reds and warm yellow-oranges. Less frequently used are *Parrotia persica, Malus tschonowskii* or *Sorbus hupehensis.* Deciduous conifers such as *Larix decidua, Ginkgo biloba* or *Metasequoia glyptostroboides* all colour well. Shrubs such as *Fothergilla, Euonymus, Rhus* and *Rhododendron luteum* show leaf colour in shades from scarlet to yellow and may be used in association with climbers for dramatic effect – *Vitis coignetiae* or *Parthenocissus tricuspidata* "Veitchii" are most suitable.

Many forms of *Clematis* bear decorative seed heads in autumn and *Clematis tangutica* produces attractive yellow lantern-shaped flowers. *Physalis, Diplacus* and *Lunaria* produce unusual seed pods and *Skimmia, Ilex, Symphoricarpos, Cotoneaster* and *Pyracantha* are all useful berry-bearing shrubs. The crab apples of *Malus* "John Downie" are amongst the largest and most profusely borne, and look good contrasted with the vivid red hips of *Rosa moyesii* "Geranium".

*Right This elegantly arched bridge spans a lake of reflected colour in the clear crisp air of autumn. Whilst many of the trees are just turning to autumnal shades, the shrub-like masses of Acer, peeping from the woodland edge, provide more brilliant colour.*

*Above The dying foliage of autumn instils a quietness into the woodland scene, accentuated by penetrating dampness and misty vapours. The vibrant colours are strong and bright, yet tinged with sadness and decay.*

*Left The geometry of the pergola is dark and strong against the cloudy sky beyond. The shady canopy opens gradually as the golden leaves of* Celastrus orbiculatus *drop to the floor. Its tracery of branches will decorate the structure until the spring and light and shade will play upon the paving beneath until the canopy regrows, restoring a shady retreat.*

# THE WINTER GARDEN

Often ericas and conifers are considered appropriate to the winter garden for their green foliage or flowers when little else is of interest. Personally, I find the scaly or spiny leaves and coarse structure of many ericaceous plants associated with heather gardens unpleasant and unsightly. Similarly, the current vogue for conifers relies heavily on variegations and dwarf forms. Their dark green foliage is often dull and sombre and their yellow-greens somehow artificial. Deciduous shrubs and trees display their stems, bark and branching forms to best effect in the winter months. *Quercus robur* and *Fagus sylvatica* retain their copper-toned leaves through winter on young growth which contrasts with the shiny spikes of *Ilex* in a tapestry-like hedge.

Use the colourful trunks of *Betula*, *Acer* and *Arbutus* against the more exciting evergreens such as *Calocedrus decurrens*, *Cupressus sempervirens*, *Picea breweriana* and *Pinus ponderosa*.

**Left** *A fern is silhouetted against reflective water with tall trees looming through winter mists beyond. Often the dead foliage of ferns, and other herbaceous perennials such as* Hosta *can decorate the garden in the winter period with gold, russet and yellow tints. Sweep dead leaves away only when their colour has faded completely.*

**Above** *Frost picks out the leaf edges of* Pernettya mucronata *and the winter sun warms to the brilliant red berries and stems, contrasting sharply against the dark green leaves.*

**Far left** *The trunk of* Betula pendula *and the weeping branches of* Salix × chrysocoma *produce most interest in this snow-covered garden. The snow-laden conifers and* Rhododendron *take on black-green shades against the stark white of the surrounding snow. The tracery beyond provides a decorative backdrop.*

**Above** *Once the worst of winter is past, spring bulbs begin to emerge from the frosted ground. The rich yellows, purples and whites of crocus shimmer amongst the grass blades, introducing broad stretches of colour to washed-out vistas.*

# THE CITY GARDEN

Today a large proportion of any country's population resides in urban areas. Towns and cities offer many attractions, but from a garden design viewpoint, the possibilities and options appear limited. The restricted space, disturbing background or neighbourhood noise, the lack of privacy and the problem of pollution all mean that the creation of a small oasis of peace and greenery is difficult, if not impossible, to achieve. In fact, there are many design options available and the challenge of a city garden has produced some of the most imaginative design solutions in gardening.

## PLANTING

Although it is possible to design a garden or terrace that is wholly reliant on hard materials for effect, in an urban space this would be a mistake. The over-riding impression of most towns and cities is their hard, man-made environment from which the green space or rural idyll provides a much sought-after relief. The soft lines and patterns of plant material, changing with the seasons keep us in touch with nature, help to relax the busy mind and provide a distraction or inspire a hobby.

Compost-filled containers or pots provide a growing medium that will support an abundance of plant material. Generally, the larger the pot, the more vigorous and healthy the plant, or the greater the variety of material capable of cultivation. The most important point is the container's ability to retain enough moisture within the soil to support plant life, without needing to be topped up daily. Ameliorants within the compost can help with this. Otherwise periods of absence, on holidays in particular, can put paid to your efforts.

Terracotta and other clay pots, although attractive, do absorb the available moisture quickly and the soil is left dry and cracked. PVC or fibreglass containers retain moisture much more efficiently, though excess water must be allowed to drain away or held in a reservoir for later use.

It is a good idea to use the cheaper or more functional PVC containers for lining much more attractive clay containers, a solution offering the best compromise between looks and efficiency. Alternatively, dense planting in containers with additional annual or seasonal planting, will cover even more unsightly pots successfully so that they become almost invisible.

Irrigation tanks can be fitted to larger containers with a filler pipe

*This garden illustrates the value of bold foliage planting to create an atmosphere of seclusion. The use of different-sized pots together with the bright red parasol add drama and colour, and the impression of sunlit space beyond the terrace is very strong.*

It is best to plant one species as a mass in one container, or different species with the same colour range or theme and to introduce bold splashes of colour rather than use just one or two plants.

Larger shrubs or spreading ground-covers and climbing plants need containers of 45-75cm (18-30in) deep to sustain their demand for moisture without constantly suffering from drought. The extra depth also means greater stability through the root system. Greater diameters are the result of greater depth in a container and the restriction of space may dictate the sparing using of containers such as these.

Small trees may also be accommodated but you need at least 90cm (3ft) or more of soil to grow them successfully. The same proportions should be adhered to with built-in containers. Often the structural masonry or brickwork can absorb the available moisture or the proximity of buildings and balconies may mean that little natural rainfall ever feeds the planting.

Combinations of different-sized pots result in sculptural masses of foliage and flower that can be changed at will. Use unusual pots in stone, terracotta or timber as a theme, in different shapes and sizes. Formality can be introduced, even on the smallest scale. Exercise restraint when choosing strongly decorative containers; they are as important as the plant material within.

The plant material itself can also be manipulated to suit the style of the garden. The more informal arrangements can abound with colour and variety of texture, erupting like a controlled explosion of green foliage, decorative stems and colourful flowers. Perennials, such as rhododendron, sumac, laurel, *Fatsia* or *Cotoneaster,* can provide the main structure. Spikes of iris, New Zealand flax *(Phormium tenax)* and cabbage palm *(Cordyline australis)* provide vertical interest or specimens, whilst intense autumn colour is provided by Japanese maple *(Acer palmatum),* the smoke tree *(Cotinus coggygria)* or Chinese witch-hazel *(Hamamelis).*

Pots of *Pelargonium,* tobacco plant *(Nicotiana),* mint *(Mentha),* miniature rose *(Rosa),* pinks *(Dianthus)* and *Fuchsia* can provide a broad spectrum of summer colour and scents with daffodil *(Narcissus),* hyacinth, crocus, *Muscari* and *Primula* producing softer shades in spring.

Bay laurels or box can introduce more formal shapes and can be grown for topiary. Architectural or geometric patterns and styles can be recreated or imitated with the fine dense texture of box in particular, which responds well to pruning.

For shaded areas, try *Hosta, Fatsia,* ivy *(Hedera)* and ferns. The climbing hydrangea *(Hydrangea petiolaris)* is useful for brightening cold dark walls.

## SPACE AND ILLUSION

The eye can be deceived by playing with perspective, by emphasizing converging lines in planting borders, using large-leaved plants adjacent to

connected to the surface. Liquid fertilizer and water can be poured into the tank, which then releases the moisture and nutrients into the soil by capillary action. Alternatively, automatic drip-feed irrigation systems can be installed around the planted area.

## PLANTING UP CONTAINERS

Small herbs for scent, or textural grasses and ground-covers, can be accommodated easily in relatively small pots, perhaps 15cm-30cm (6-12in) deep. Annuals and colourful bedding plants can be grown in similar depths.

*Right The timber decking helps to relate the hard materials of the house to the densely planted garden. The walls play an important part in this softening effect, supporting climbing plants such as* Clematis, Hedera *and* Parthenocissus. *The planting drops vertically down to ground level to create depth and height, and the variegated leaf of* Hedera helix *"Glacier" breaks the monotony of green.*

*Left This compact roof-top garden uses timber both for decorative effect and to increase privacy. The pergola construction allows climbing foliage to drape and cover from above. Movable containers introduce summer or exotic bedding species, which may be taken indoors or into a conservatory over the winter period.*

the house or in the foreground and small-leaved plants in the distance or towards the end of the garden. Whites, greys and blues appear distant and reds or yellow appear stronger and closer.

Ornament or sculpture can be used as a focal point to draw the eye into the imagined distance, whilst trellis can frame or direct the eye. *Trompe l'oeil* can deceive with the illusion of space or activity beyond the garden. Mirrors can also be used to reflect the surrounding boscage and hint at a space beyond.

## POLLUTION

It is difficult to escape the effects of noise pollution in an urban setting. There is no obvious way to combat this problem as planting has very little effect as a noise screen. It can obscure the source of the noise from general view. Usually, what cannot be seen or identified is more easily ignored unless the noise is particularly disturbing.

A much more ingenious method is to introduce a distraction creating its own noise, the most appropriate source being moving water. The splashes and gurgles provide a sound source much closer to the ear than traffic or background interference, and they are also much more acceptable and pleasant.

Industrial or air-borne pollution is impossible to eradicate and can severely affect plant material. The simple answer is to use those plants that tolerate fumes, salts and toxic deposits. Roses are generally capable of tolerating quite severe pollution and deciduous species can eliminate toxic wastes when losing their leaves. Trees are superb filters for pollutants and air-borne dust, and they also replenish oxygen in the atmosphere.

## PRIVACY AND SHELTER

Privacy may be difficult to achieve in a space that is overlooked by neighbouring houses on all sides. Screening with climber-covered trellis may help in proximity to the house. Otherwise, pergolas when clothed with climbing plants can promote an overhead canopy under which you can entertain, dine or simply relax with a good book.

Take care when planting climbers. The immediate vicinity of walls and buildings is usually very dry. Plant at least 45cm (18in) away from the structure to allow the roots to seek moisture successfully. Climbers can be pruned and trimmed into shape as an alternative to rampant uncontrolled growth. Pyracantha is particularly useful in this respect as it can be closely trimmed and shaped. It also flowers profusely and produces rich red or orange berries in autumn. Virginia creeper also provides a vivid display of fiery red leaves that drop to reveal a delicate tracery against the stone or brickwork.

## A CHELSEA ROOF GARDEN, LONDON

With restricted space and little or no usable topsoil, the city garden presents a formidable challenge to the gardener. But with the judicious use of pots and containers, dense jungles of foliage and flower can be produced, seemingly out of nowhere. This roof garden is an excellent example of just what can be achieved. The colour and excitement of the planting really cannot be beaten and the restricted views and pathways make the garden seem far larger than it really is.

Decorative balustrades and tree canopies help to provide pleasant enclosure but the plants themselves have been carefully chosen to hide boundaries, edges and views, giving an illusion of size and scale. The pathways have been left relatively clear of decoration and the planting has been deliberately pushed back to form a wall of ornamental boscage.

*Left* The delicate leaf of Sambucus racemosa *"Plumosa Aurea" decorates the densely packed border planting with its attractive dissected shapes.* Phlox paniculata, Ruta graveolens *and* Berberis thunbergii *"Aurea" make a successful, if unlikely, combination beneath.*

*Above* The turned finials on the balustrade uprights make a nice finishing detail. The rich planting on either side belies the fact that this is a roof garden, while the mature plane tree beyond gives a curious sense of scale.*

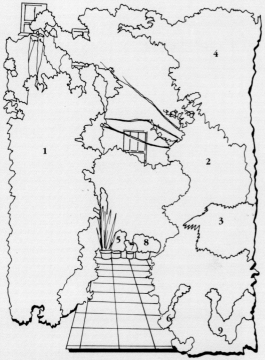

## SCHEME FOR A CITY GARDEN

*1 Lavatera thuringiaca* "Rosea"
*2 Rosa* "Scarlet Fire"
*3 Acer palmatum* "Dissectum Nigrum"
*4 Prunus cerasifera* "Pissardii"
*5 Pelargonium* × *hortorum*
*6 Salpiglossis sinuata*
*7 Impatiens walleriana*
*8 Begonia elatior* hybrid
*9 Tradescantia* × *andersoniana*

**Left** *In summer the roof garden becomes
a mini jungle of foliage . Pots
provide summer interest, and can be
moved around the garden to provide
extra colour.*

# SURFACE TREATMENTS

When introducing hard materials into the garden take account of the existing character of the surrounding buildings and neighbourhood. Look to see which material predominates and try to match it, at least in colour, or alternatively use a contrast in texture or colour, or shape and size. Take a look also at the scale of the property and at the boundary treatment. These two elements will enclose the garden, physically creating the space and probably dominating it. Examine the window and door positions and note any decorative feature on the property that might suggest a matching material or that could inspire a pattern for its paving design. In a small space, keep the paving simple, restricted to one or two materials, and make sure any decorative walling and steps, or structures such as a pergola, arch or loggia, are kept to a minimum.

**Far left** *The successful transformation of this awkward space stems from the restrained use of paving materials and the restricted formal use of planting, allowing the elements themselves to provide the decoration. The brickwork is used as a backdrop full of oatmeal colour, leaving the subdued gravel and timber decking to create pattern and texture. Had the change of level been created in timber or in timber-retained gravel it might have produced a more homogeneous result.*

**Left** *The unifying elements of this complicated design are the paving and the planting. The terracotta tones run through the paving, walls and containers. The predominantly dark green planting is highlighted only by one or two patches of yellow-green and by the rich texture of foliage. The paving pattern is a kind of basket-weave, which produces an intricate threadlike texture across the surface. The main contrast in the garden springs from the ochre-red of the brickwork and terracotta, draped with the rich green foliage. The clipped evergreens, fountain and seating area provide focal points within the space.*

**Above** *This circular terrace provides ample space for sunbathing and for decorative potted plants. The stone slabs are full of colour with a strong jointing pattern emphasized in light mortar. The circular shape is strengthened by the red brick edging, which neatens off the stone slabs. Smaller units, such as brick or stone sets, are much more suitable for circular or intricate shapes; large slabs need a great deal of cutting and shaping to fit. The brick and terracotta pots complement each other well and the architectural plant material in grey-green provides interest and punctuation. The much darker background foliage beyond emphasizes the brightness of the terrace, underlining its attraction as a place for entertaining or relaxing under the sun.*

# RAISED SURFACES

Even within a relatively restricted space a change of level brings interest and relief. Spaces, either elevated or sunken, are endowed with a special quality which sets them apart. The physical or psychological change which stairs, steps or ramps engender is inescapable. Areas defined by changes of level are thus special or different, and activities may be introduced specifically tailored to these different zones. Raised terraces may become outside dining rooms. Sunken areas could accommodate a child's sand pit or an ornamental pool. Privacy or secrecy could be created in hidden corners or elevated balconies used to celebrate public display. Even steps themselves can be accentuated, either in a purely functional capacity or as decorative terraces furnished with containers, balustrades, lighting or ornament. Ramps not only allow important access around the garden for the infirm or the disabled but give a softer less dynamic character to changes of level. Raised planting beds enhance the difference in height and dramatic changes of level can be emphasized by trailing or climbing plant material. The excitement of moving water is also enhanced by dropping through a series of levels, creating noise and movement. If you introduce different paving patterns or materials at a change of level, it gives the impression of entering a new or separate space. Level changes can be used like layers of skin peeled back to reveal a new surface beneath or as in an archaeological dig where beautiful mosaics suddenly appear below layers of mundane materials.

*Right* The decorative foliage and changes of level hide the children's play area from general view. The brick is warm and interesting in itself and the shadow line from the steps combined with its sculptural effect on vertical surfaces make this small scheme very successful.

*Left* The textures of pebbles, boulders, timber and concrete work well in this arrangement. The plant material is separated and given added significance by the change of level, albeit small. The timber used is old railway sleepers, durable and relatively low-cost. They often take on an appearance of stone from their long-term contact with track ballast.

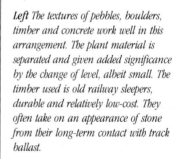

**Below** *The focal point in this garden is given extra importance by its position on a higher level. The use of timber decking to achieve the additional height also marks a transition from the lower level of brick paving. Enclosure is provided by planting and the steps are also used to display plant material in containers.*

# CONTAINER PLANTING

Plant containers are ideal for city gardens, which are often raised terraces, balconies or roof-tops. Introduce a range of container shapes and sizes to add interest. Terracotta pots with moulded or applied embellishments are a favourite, weathering over time and attracting lichen and algae. Their ochre tones contrast well with draping ground-covers and their hand-crafted character complements the precise architecture of *Cordyline, Agave* or *Yucca.* Other suitable materials for containers include timber (which can be stained hardwood or painted softwood) and stone.

Pre-cast concrete could be used but rarely has any decorative or aesthetic quality. Fibreglass or plastic liners may be used inside porous containers to help with moisture retention. You need to ensure there is adequate drainage from the pot – with weep holes and a gravel layer in the base. Use different shapes and sizes together, and fill them with plants of different character – dense evergreen ground-cover or colourful annuals, architectural shapes against decorative foliage. Use bark clippings, pea shingle, pebbles or gravel to add interest to the surface of the container and to prevent evaporation and weed growth and leave some attractive pots empty, purely for decoration.

## PLANTS FOR POTS

Few plants are truly suitable for containers, which form an artificial environment that depends on care and maintenance. However, strong architectural plants work well, such as *Cordyline*, *Phormium*, and *Yucca*. For more foliage interest try *Fatsia japonica*, *Mahonia* or *Viburnum* with *Camellia*, *Choisya ternata* and *Hibiscus* providing flower. Introduce annuals such as *Impatiens, Lobelia, Alyssum* and *Pelargonium* perhaps set amongst ground-cover species such as *Hedera, Alchemilla mollis* or *Helxine*, which trail or drape down to ground level. Climbing plants may also be contained in large pots to drape pergolas or decorate bare walls. Use *Wisteria, Parthenocissus, Rosa* or *Hydrangea* alongside wall-hugging shrubs such as *Fremontodendron, Garrya* or *Ceanothus*, which prefer the protection of walls and fences.

**Far left** *The hard materials of this city garden are softened by the rich textures of* Cordyline, Fatsia japonica *and* Cyperus. *The terracotta pots introduce a warmth of tone, echoed in the soft pink of the enclosing wall, which acts as a perfect screen for strong shadow effects.*

**Left** *The dynamic but stark architecture, reflective and brilliant, gleams against a sun-filled sky. The planting brings welcome relief, in the relaxing greens of* Ficus benjamina *and exuberant sunlit magenta flowers of* Bougainvillea. *The organic texture of timber and the earthen quality of terracotta help to subdue the man-made environment.*

# VERTICAL PLANTING

As space is often so restricted in urban gardens the use of the vertical plane provides a rich source of decorative effects. Privacy is usually an important requirement and the ability to shelter, hide or cover space with trellis-work or pergolas clothed in plant material is much valued. Bare house walls of brick or concrete also need softening and densely branching climbers can transform them with intricate foliage and contoured depth. Climbers are not the only answer to breaking the sterility of vertical walls or screens. Wall-loving shrubs can be used such as garrya *(Garrya elliptica)*, ceanothus *(Ceanothus × "Gloire de Versailles")* or fremontia *(Fremontia californica)*. Use white-painted softwood trellis to create geometric patterns or use dark-stained frames to allow the plant material to dominate. Decorate with finials or ornamental flourishes which peep through climbing foliage.

**Left** *The bold grid of this trellis-work is accentuated by the white-painted finish. Decorative green foliage works well against such a framework which, although structural and definite, still allows views into the other sections of garden. Few climbing plants are needed against this support as its clean lines and emphatic pattern are inherently decorative.*

**Above** *These functional steps and balustrade are enlived by the vivid colour of cascading plant material. The tufted ground-covering potential of thrift* (Armeria caespitosa) *is fully realized in this situation where dry-sun-loving species are required. Small containers have been built onto the end of each step to accommodate this planting.*

### *SUITABLE CLINGING AND TWINING PLANTS*

Climbing plants may be easily divided into self-clinging species or twining vine-like growers. The former include ivies such as *Hedera helix*, *H. colchica* or *H. canariensis*, climbing hydrangea *(Hydrangea petiolaris)* and *Parthenocissus henryana* or *P. tricuspidata*. *Trachelospermum* is also self-clinging. The latter group covers the majority of climbing plants which need some kind of frame or trellis for support. When erecting climber supports allow space between the wall and trellis to enable twining branches or tendrils to gain support. Use clematis *(Clematis montana, C. tangutica* or *C. orientalis)* for smaller blooms or *C.* "Mrs Cholmondeley", *C.* "Marie Boisselot" or *C.* "Lasurstern" for larger flowers often up to 15cm (6in) in diameter. Use wisteria in purple or white forms *(Wisteria sinensis),* honeysuckle *(Lonicera periclymenum)* or jasmine *(Jasminum officinale)* for scent. For a more exotic appearance try passion flower *(Passiflora caerulea),* trumpet vine *(Campsis radicans),* Chilean glory flower *(Eccremocarpus scaber)* or *Cobaea scandens. Tropaeolum, Actinidia, Vitis* and *Hedera* are all useful for foliage effect.

*Left The vertical surface of this wall has been virtually covered with the rich textured foliage of hop* (Humulus lupulus), *large-flowering hybrid clematis and wisteria* (Wisteria sinensis). *This vivid display can easily cover or disguise sterile or unpleasant vertical surfaces and provide an interesting backdrop to further decorative border or container planting.*

# THE WILD GARDEN

As human pressures destroy the landscape around us the idea of a wild garden, in which plants and animals are shielded from the ravages of progress, grows in popularity and value. The idea is not new.

William Robinson and Gertrude Jekyll were responsible at the turn of the century for stimulating moves away from rigid planting plans and formal designs. Their use of native and species plants in woodlands and flowering borders created a novel aura of disorder, impressionistic mixes of colour and exuberant nature.

Although their work was inspiring and influential, the wild gardens that have developed recently are quite different – flowering meadows, dark, still, ponds with floating lilies and spiky rushes, damp bogs with golden marsh marigolds and quiet woodlands with bustling verges and clearings. These elements all, of course, occur naturally and even if you think they are impossible to recreate on the garden scale, the opposite is true.

Ecologists would argue that intensively mown lawns are sterile and unimaginative compared with the alternative of a colourful, easily maintained, species-rich environment, otherwise known as the meadow.

The associations of grasses and flowering plants give the meadows their romantic connotations. The picture of poppies swaying in corn fields and verges (not strictly meadows) is evocative of warm hazy summer days, their vivid scarlet and dusty gold sympathetic to the sultry atmosphere. Snakeshead fritillary lends a more sinister beauty to the water meadow with its quivering snake-like flowers. These decorative blooms are set amidst the fine emerald spikes of grasses, expressing the movement of the wind waving their delicate seed-heads.

A meadow can be recreated on the scale of the garden lawn, without the well-manicured lawn being squeezed out altogether. The mowing regime adopted can allow fine ornamental turf to co-exist alongside longer grass verges containing the meadow species. Borders, pathways and lawn areas are easily created, harsh lines are eliminated and the effect is subtle but effective. Strimming machines allow you to cut the grass to any height but the timing of the cut is important.

Daffodils and other spring bulbs rejuvenate by drawing strength from their leaves, which should not be cut back for some time after flowering. Late spring and early summer flowers must be allowed to finish their flowering

*Delicate poppy heads decorate the European countryside with fluttering crimson petals, often waving in the golden haze of cornfields, as if in some impressionist painting. As seeds are brought to the surface they explode and grow, eventually producing lantern-like heads in late summer.*

cycle so that those that set seed may do so, thus ensuring continuity for the next season. The same applies to late summer flowers.

## WOODLAND EDGE

Many of the species associated with meadows and grassland adapt to the fringes of woodland, scrub and hedgerows or field boundaries. The intermingling of field and woodland plants provides a species-rich community which crosses the boundary between full and deep shade.

Here tiny mounds of spring primroses *(Primula vulgaris)* are followed by towering spikes of pink-freckled foxglove *(Digitalis purpurea)*. Flowering thorn species *(Crataegus)* and viburnums tangle with scrambling roses, honeysuckle *(Lonicera)* and clematis, their simple flowers providing elegant alternatives to often over-embellished garden varieties.

Groups of small trees, appropriate to the garden scale, such as birch *(Betula)* or alder *(Alnus)* offer spring catkins and flickering summer shade. If space allows, a small copse can provide a woodland effect. This transition zone between field and wood can be easily compressed into a community of plants only 5 to 10cm (2-4in) across.

The cool relaxing shade of a mature woodland is most welcome in the

warmest times of the year but the woodland itself is probably the most difficult habitat to recreate. Time is the overriding factor which matures and enriches the woodland scene. The understorey or lower layer of vegetation is adapted to heavy shade and thrives in the undisturbed backwaters of the forest. Here bluebells *(Endymion non-scriptus)* dog's mercury, bird's nest orchids, wood sorrel and wood anemone *(Anemone)* thrive, identifying ancient woodland and creating a mystique of their own.

Man's intervention with coppicing or clearing encourages a rich flush of vegetation that was previously dormant and suddenly desperate to soak up the sunlight.

## WATER

The inclusion of water in the wild garden is essential. Even the smallest pool is capable of supporting plants from a variety of water habitats. Water lilies *(Nymphaea)* float serenely on the surface of a pond while their roots plummet to invisible depths below. Marginal plants such as iris, water mint *(Mentha aquatica)*, and water forget-me-not *(Myosotis palustris)* escape from the pond bed. The marsh marigold *(Caltha palustris)* or ragged robin brighten dank bog planting before dry land is regained.

Butyl liners or pre-fabricated pond liners are relatively cheap and are ideal for sealing porous ground to allow water to collect to form small pools. It is surprising how quickly such man-made elements are colonized by flora and fauna to provide one of the most satisfying and interesting of ecosystems.

## WILD ANIMALS

The creation of wild habitats should attract wildlife immediately. Indigenous plants provide basic foodstuffs – berries, nectar, seeds and nuts – creating the shelter and protection necessary for nesting or burrowing animals.

For most garden owners it is exciting and fulfilling to provide such shelter for a variety of birds and mammals, bringing us closer to nature. Wildlife activity identifies the passage of the seasons as birds return to nest, hedgehogs sniff and poke for food after their long hibernation and the air is filled with the buzzing drone of bees or the brilliant flashes of darting dragonflies enjoying the warmth of the summer sun. Decaying vegetation or wood in discreet piles will encourage insect life which in turn attracts birds.

Allowing the odd nettle patch to thrive or introducing buddleia, brambles, viburnum, mint and lavender into the borders will attract butterflies and bees. Although native species are attractive to and valuable for wildlife, exotic annuals and shrubs will not detract from the wild quality of the garden if used sympathetically. The tobacco plant *(Nicotiana)* provides a profuse display of soft colour throughout the summer with a sweet fragrance unmatched on warm evenings.

**Right** *The black trunks and branches of olive trees* (Olea europaea) *spread out above a wild flower meadow below. The soft sunlit colours introduce a timeless quality reminiscent of less intensive farming methods of years gone by.*

**Left** *An exuberant mix of foliage pattern and filigree light and shade makes this woodland floor rich in colour and texture. Fine grasses, ferns and shrubs cover the ground in an* ad hoc *mixture, whilst light penetrates the canopy in camouflage shapes.*

**Far left** *A complex arrangement of colour and texture introduce a wild character to this mass of planting.* Lysimachia *and* Lilium *boast vivid colour against the finer variegated texture of* Phalaris arundinacea *"Picta"*

## SEMI-WILD WOODLAND AND WATER GARDEN, SURREY, ENGLAND

Transformed from a wilderness into an attractive semi-wild garden, this four-acre site incorporates two lakes as well as a large expanse of mature woodland. The owners, who spend a lot of time abroad, wanted a garden style that retained the natural charm of the heavily wooded site, as well as one which would look after itself while they were away on business. There are no flower beds as such in this garden, which relies for its charm on a judicious balance between nature and artifice. The wild plants, including pink campions, foxgloves, bluebells, primroses and cowslips, thrive in the clearings between the trees and the native and species plants – in the main large-leaved moisture-loving plants like rheums, ligularias and so on – jostle together companionably at the waterside and woodland edges. Ferns do particularly well in the shady areas between wood and lake, and make an attractive linking device between the wilder and more cultivated parts of the garden. To keep a successful planting balance on the woodland floor, the trees need to be thinned periodically to allow light through their canopies.

**Above** *The decorative flowers of* Rhododendron *brighten this woodland garden for spring effect with delicate hues of bluebell* (Endymion non-scriptus) *and campion* (Silene dioica) *decorating the long grasses beneath.*

**Right** *This overgrown pathway invites us to explore the mysteries of the woodland garden. The lush foliage beneath is bold and fleshy with delicate ferns pushing upward, suggestive of damp forest clearings, where sunlight filters through.*

## SCHEME FOR A WILD GARDEN

*1 Acer palmatum*
*2 Crataegus oxyacantha "Paul's Scarlet"*
*3 Silene dioica*
*4 Dryopteris filix-mas*

*5 Rodgersia podophylla*
*6 Lonicera japonica "Halliana"*
*7 Astilboides tabularis*

**Left** *The moss-covered steps lead tantalizingly up into the woodland beyond as if to some long-forgotten land. The fine textures of woodland grasses and herbs are striped with shadow from the canopy overhead and glow with filtered sunshine.*

# FLOWERING MEADOWS

Flowering meadows are romantic, evocative and rapidly disappearing. But as an alternative to the formal lawn meadows have a great deal of character and by incorporating them into your garden you are offering refuge to species which might otherwise be in danger of dying out. A "cultivated" meadow can become relatively species-rich and a wide variety of insects and birds could eventually grow to depend on such a garden as a sanctuary or food source. The idyllic look of the wild meadow is not as easy to achieve or maintain as you might suppose, because the flowering plants which are the essential ingredient of the wild meadow do not flower at the same time of the year. The management of the meadow becomes a balancing act, as those species which flower early in the season should be cut down only from midsummer onwards. Species that produce flowers in late summer should be cut in early autumn. To achieve the right effect the meadow is not usually cut until early summer; if no cutting is carried out at all then the more vigorous grasses will take over from all other species but if the meadow is cut too regularly then the rigours of a more formal regime apply and the flowering plants suffer. These regular but infrequent mowings allow the flowers to set seed before they are cut, for what was traditionally a hay crop. Although it is possible to combine the two crops of flowers in one meadow the best solution, if you have the space, is to have different seasonal meadows. Alternatively use flowering verges around a more formal lawn. This style is particularly suitable some distance from the house where less formal treatments are appropriate.

*Left The fine structure of the long grass verge is visible at the edge of the more formal lawn. Beyond the divide, tall herbs such as* Ranunculus *and* Heracleum mantegazzianum *emerge from a soft cloud of seed-heads. Hedgerow planting beyond provides an informal backdrop and the dead tree stump offers an attractive haven for grubs and insects. Later in the year the verge should be cut down or strimmed, leaving the grass on the surface to dry and the flowers to drop their seed.*

*Above The crimson tissue-paper-like petals of the common poppy* (Papaver rhoeas) *flutter on a steep coastal slope, their warm colour contrasting with the cool blue sea. These flowers require soil disturbance in order to thrive, hence their association with arable farming. The cultivation of soil brings dormant seeds to the surface and their summer life-cycle begins. The lantern-like seed-heads are a most attractive feature, tipping tiny seeds out as the wind blows. They are often dried for decoration.*

The basic structure of a meadow relies on grass species. Less vigorous species should be used with finer leaves than the dominating *Lolium perenne* (rye grass). *Agrostis tenuis* (common bent), *Festuca rubra* (red fescue) and *Poa pratensis* (smooth meadow grass) are all useful and other species may include *Alopecurus pratensis* (meadow foxtail), *Phleum pratense* (purple-stem cat's-tail) and *Cynosurus cristatus* (crested dog's tail). Use *Anthoxanthum odoratum* (sweet vernal-grass) to provide a strong new-mown hay smell when harvested. For the spring-flowering meadow, include *Sanguisorba minor* (salad burnet), *Rhinanthus minor* (yellow rattle), *Prunella vulgaris* (selfheal) and *Cardamine pratensis* (cuckoó flower). *Primula veris* (cowslip) and *Fritillaria meleagris* (snake's-head fritillary) are also suitable. For summer effect use *Hypericum perforatum* (perforate St John's-wort), *Malva moschata* (musk mallow) or *Campanula rotundifolia* (harebell). *Ranunculus acris* (meadow buttercup), *Centaurea nigra* (common knapweed) and *Leucanthemum vulgare* (oxeye daisy) can also be included.

**Left** *The flowers of* Leucanthemum vulgare *dot the meadow grass like bright confetti left over from a wedding party. Their cheerful yellow and white heads are evocative of summer days in idyllic heat-hazed landscapes. Between the flowers and grasses, orchids seek the sunshine. The decorative border beyond the meadow complements the flowery mead with clouds of white* Gypsophila *and spikes of foxglove (*Digitalis*).*

# THE NATURAL GARDEN

Once the rigours of high-maintenance gardens with clean soil and sterile lawns are disregarded, nature can be given the upper hand in influencing planting design. With relaxed control, plants can be allowed to self-seed, lawns to admit wild flowers and grass verges to run into wild hedgerows.

Mow short pathways through meadows or woodlands to create routes or a directional emphasis. Edges can simply be identified by longer verge grass. Herbs and flowers such as *Endymion, Silene, Anemone* and *Primula* may lead into a shrub layer of *Corylus, Viburnum* or *Euonymus*.

For terrace areas introduce plants which scatter seed in all directions. *Digitalis, Papaver, Nigella* and *Alyssum* will all self-seed easily. By reducing hoeing and border maintenance, particularly in spring, these plants will thrive and spread again. Crevices and joints in paving will be filled with foliage and colour as the garden advances towards the house.

Allow hedgerow species to invade the garden and reduce pruning on more formal hedges, introducing instead the wild dog rose *(Rosa canina)*, *Lonicera periclymenum, Viburnum opulus* or *Sambucus nigra*. Use *Crataegus monogyna* for flower and berry interest, which will in turn attract wildlife in the form of birds, insects and small mammals.

*Left* This sunfilled woodland glade is rich in herbs and wild flowers peeping through knee-high grasses and foliage. The formal lawn can be allowed to stretch to the woodland edge where the longer herb layer starts. Alternatively, pathways may be mown through this layer to allow visitors to explore or to discover the decorative trees and shrubs above.

*Above* Narcissus *and* Iberis *invade the pathway, taking advantage of the high light levels before the tree canopy closes in full leaf. The random stone paving allows moss and* Forget-me-not (Myosotis) *to invade freely.*

*Right* Invading plants disguise the edges of borders and the beginning of paving in this dreamy, overgrown terrace. The fairytale appearance is not the result of neglect but of allowing plants to self-seed, introducing ground-cover into paving and using plants which are commonly thought of as weeds.

# WILD WATER GARDENS

The creation of a wild water feature introduces an interesting range of wildlife into the garden. A standing pool of still, reflective water is the most appropriate feature to introduce into a wild garden; fountains or waterfalls are too artificial or contrived in appearance. For those lucky enough to have a natural stream or river running through their land, experiment with changes of level, damming parts into still pools or incorporating bog areas. Fast streams, with swift currents and disturbing eddies, may be too violent to support aquatic plant material. In cases like these, concentrate on the bankside planting associations with fine grasses such as *Festuca*, *Molinia* or *Deschampsia*, under overhanging branches of a multi-stemmed *Betula pendula* or *Alnus glutinosa*. Shade, texture, drifts of colour, stripy reeds and hummocks of moss, with the vivid yellow of *Caltha palustris* in the damp marginal areas, are all useful elements.

*Below The dense shade, dramatic foliage and contrasting textures seen here are typical of waterside planting. What would otherwise be used as ornamental plant material can be mixed together in rich associations to give a wild, jungle-like appearance, countering the smooth gloss of the pool surface. Primula japonica makes a welcome splash of colour with its handsome heads of flowers held aloft on tall, delicate stems.*

*Left Twisted or fallen tree trunks add reflected drama to the water margins and invite us to explore their precarious delights. Dead wood left to rot is a rich source of insect life in the garden, establishing a source of food for other wild animals. Polygonum bistorta thrusts its pink brush-like flowers through dense ground-covering foliage, enjoying the dampness of this water's edge.*

*Right The pool is almost hidden in dense undergrowth but comes as a refreshing surprise to the hot, sun-filled colour of the meadow. Hard edges to wild water features such as this would be completely inappropriate. The waterline should be indefinite or incidental, rather than contrived or applied.*

# WOODLAND FLOWERS

The woodland floor can be a sterile, dark area with little plant material of interest. Beech leaves emit a poison which kills off their own seedlings and stifles competition, and the ground beneath coniferous woodland is simply carpeted with dead needles. However, given an opening in the foliage canopy overhead or a clearing brought about by nature or by man, the woodland floor bursts into life and dormant seedlings take full advantage of warm sunshine and rain. This is one reason for the wealth and diversity of species found in a coppiced woodland. Gaps in the trees therefore allow light to percolate into the heart of the forest and the herbaceous and shrub layer thrives. As the coppiced stools grow and close in again, so the lower levels of vegetation fade and disappear. It is important with wild woodland to maintain this kind of ecosystem. By planting ornamental woodland species a relatively instant effect of rich vegetation is achieved. With native plants the problem is not so easily solved. Some species enjoy dappled or part-shade, some deep shade, and some direct light. These conditions may all be found in mature woodland but when starting a wood from nothing, you will find that the young trees cast very little shade at all and full sunlight pervades your would-be forest. Many herb species such as wood sorrel *(Oxalis acetosella)* would die out in newly-planted woods.

*Below The fabulous blue of bluebells* (Endymion non-scriptus) *catches the spirit of spring in fresh green woodlands. They represent a sudden flash of inspirational colour before the canopy closes overhead and the quiet darkness of leafy shade takes over. These plants are widely available in a variety of colours but the blue is still the best. Do not be tempted to dig them up from their positions in the wild – it is strictly illegal.*

*Left A woodland edge of rough grass catches enough spring sunshine to burst into colour.* Primula veris × vulgaris *is a hybrid between the cowslip and the primrose, often found where they grow together.* Fritillaria meleagris *and* Pulsatilla vulgaris *share a common purple and a solitary* Muscari *creeps in alongside.* Anemone nemorosa *is one of the most delicately beautiful woodland flowers and looks best planted in drifts or masses.*

### SOME SHADE LOVERS

For woodland flowers which cover the ground use primrose *(Primula vulgaris)*, bluebells *(Endymion non-scriptus)*, wood anemones *(Anemone nemorosa)* or wood sorrel *(Oxalis acetosella)*. For foliage plants try ivy *(Hedera helix)* which enjoys quite heavy shade. *H. h.* "Hibernica" has much larger leaves than common ivy but still looks "natural". The wild strawberry *Fragaria vesca,* is a little more delicate and *Ranunculus ficaria, Lamium maculatum album* or *Geranium sylvaticum* are also appropriate. *Narcissus pseudonarcissus* provides a taller golden flower and *Allium ursinum* has white onion-like flowers. Beware of the smell however; this is known as wild garlic (or Ramson's) and has a pungent, but not unpleasant, odour. Foxglove *(Digitalis purpurea)* will provide tall spikes of flower ranging in colour from white through to a dark purple-red. *Silene dioica* has smaller flowers in perfect foxglove tones and *Geranium robertianum* is virtually a miniature version. Snowdrops *(Galanthus nivalis)* and lily-of-the-valley *(Convallaria majalis)* provide white flowers to match.

**Left** *The elegant heads of* Digitalis purpurea *stand out against the shade beyond. They are most attractive to bees which disappear into their freckled bells. Later their spikes bear hundreds of tiny seeds which are sprinkled into the air. The plants are biennials and so will not appear in the same position year after year.*

# THE AL FRESCO GARDEN

The garden is effectively a room outside. In warm climates the area around the house can be used to the full and is often seen as an extension of the interior space. In temperate zones, where the weather is less predictable, the ideal may prove difficult to realize, but the concept of *al fresco* living still remains most appealing.

The interface between interior and exterior is one of the richest sources of design options now that technology allows whole walls to be glazed, often with sliding screens to allow free circulation of air and light. This effectively brings the garden space into the living room or vice versa.

### THE GARDEN ROOM

To use the external space as a living room requires careful planning. You are creating an area that will probably become the most heavily used section of the entire garden. Paving of some description must be used to withstand wear, to provide a firm base for furniture, to allow children to play, to entertain guests, and for sunbathing or simply for decoration. Furniture can be introduced in a variety of styles, complemented by decorative pots, ornaments or sculpture.

Sand pits, water pipes or specialized play equipment can allow children to play in proximity to the house under a watchful eye. Trellis screens encourage plants to climb, creating green walls, enclosing a more private sheltered space or sun trap. Lighting can extend the hours of use on warm evenings when a cooling breeze brings relief.

### PAVING

The variety of paving materials now available makes choice difficult. Cheaper materials such as concrete, timber or gravel do not necessarily mean a shorter functional life or a second-rate appearance compared with more expensive stone, brick or tiles.

The important design criteria are to be honest to the chosen material and to avoid over-decoration. Beware of using imitation stone or brick. These materials, usually textured or patterned concrete, are artificially dyed or decorated to resemble a more expensive or natural material. The concrete weathers differently, dyes fade and the end result can be drab and grey.

*The garden should be filled with spaces which invite discovery and enjoyment, whether intimate and informal or dramatic and formal. Dining here would certainly be a pleasure over the summer months with tantalizing glimpses of the garden beyond.*

*Left This pool presents a focal point within the garden for entertaining guests or for simple relaxation. The planting and rock garden screen the pool from prying eyes and provide a sheltered area for sunbathing.*

*Far right The clean, classical shapes of this swimming pool need no decoration or softening by plant material. The cream-white stone, formal lawn and turquoise water are refreshing to see without any further complication. The white Lutyens bench and parasol complete a theatrical arrangement which demands attention and invites enjoyment.*

*Below A more intimate entertaining space is identified by the simple dark-stained pergola and formal paving beneath. The planting extends and decorates the structures, embellishing it with colour and texture. The simple surfaces of lawn and paving exaggerate the richness of the plant material which explodes from every border.*

Use a material for its own inherent quality. Use concrete for its versatility, and for its texture when the aggregate is decoratively exposed. Use brick and stone for their patina, weathering potential, surface textures and organic colours: blue engineering brick and slate for their iridescent purples and lustrous surfaces, granite for its sparkling quartz and marble for its veined richness. Gravel and cobbles or pebbles give a more textured surface in contrast and are extremely flexible.

Timber decking offers a more organic surface that can be stained or, with hardwoods, left to weather to a silvery grey. Terracotta or clay tiles can be moulded or laid in decorative shapes and colours.

Avoid over-decoration, particularly in small areas which can easily look fussy. Restrict combinations of materials to two or three at the most. Paving patterns can easily become samplers where no real choice is made and a patchwork of colour and texture results. Allow plants and flowers to decorate, and use the paving to contrast.

Planting should be bold and decorative in proximity to the house and terrace in order to relate to the predominating architectural style and geometry.

Colour, scent and texture are all important elements to be considered. The area will be seen or used much more than other sections of the garden.

### POTS AND PLANTING

*Phormium,* bamboo, *Fatsia, Hosta, Rodgersia* and *Cordyline* are all inherently architectural and strong. Many of the grass species such as *Miscanthus* or *Phalaris* also possess these qualities and, matched with textural ground-covers draping or creeping over boundaries and edges, the effect is luxuriant and bold.

Flowers such as rose, iris, magnolia or lily are all elegantly structured. They can be contrasted with simpler shapes such as rock rose, camellia, poppy or clematis. They can be introduced incidentally in a border, to be admired by visitors or enjoyed when the terrace is in use. Alternatively, whole areas of planting can be colour-themed using the rich palette of flower pigments. Annuals or biennials are often best restricted to pots and containers, as their colours are often so vivid and strong. Containers are versatile and can be moved around at will or arranged in a sculptural group.

Chinese or Japanese urns, and Mediterranean terracotta or ceramic planters furnish the open air room, though their frost resistance is an important consideration before purchase. Antique stone or lead may be more dependable and sculptural. One or two in a contemporary setting can work as a magnificent contrast.

Sculptural works or artefacts may also be introduced to punctuate the space or to act as a dramatic focal point. It is important to create a setting for pieces of art with planting or paving, otherwise the pieces can look foreign and out of place.

### FURNITURE

Furnishing the outdoor room can be difficult, depending on the climate. Generally the idea of living or dining out-of-doors is a celebration of the open air; festive, exciting and romantic, no matter how frequently you enjoy it.

Elegant reclining seats or liner chairs in stained timber can be moved around the terrace to follow the sun, or to take advantage of a quiet corner. Heavy benches or built-in seats are restrictive and static. The enjoyment of the entire space is important and changes of mood can mean that you want to enjoy the sun one day and shade the next.

### SPECIAL EFFECTS

Subdued lighting in creamy white or yellows will enhance the atmosphere after dark. Be careful with spotlights as bad positioning can lead to glare and while they can effectively wash an area with light, they can also distract. Low-level lighting angled on the floor can produce startling effects. The ground surface is clearly illuminated to pick out steps or obstacles but the planting then creates dramatic shadows, adding excitement. Spotlights can be lost in the undergrowth or uplighters may be used to pick out the tracery of a small tree or specimen plant against the velvet blue of the night sky.

Changes of level can also introduce interest. Steps can delineate and identify the boundaries of a garden space, acting as a transition zone into another area. Raised planting beds can also identify a space and introduce a vertical enclosure similar to that of an indoor room. Climbing or ground-cover plants can be used to drape and tumble over the coping, dripping down the wall and onto the terrace. Unless the planter walls are softened in this way, the effect of bare structures is sterile and artificial. Screens and trellis-work can enhance the vertical elements and decoration in terms of strong grid patterns or delicate filigree can be introduced.

Sand pits, splash pools or trickle fountains can provide a facility close enough to the house for children to play freely under observation. Unstructured play facilities are much more appropriate for children, allowing them to discover or experiment without the rigid limitations of climbing frames. Swings, ropes, nets and hide-aways can each be accommodated within a small space. Water is fun to play with and a trickle fountain which drains rather than collects in a pool is both safe and decorative.

## AN OPEN-AIR POOL GARDEN, MELBOURNE, AUSTRALIA

The ideal climate for *al fresco* living is warm, sunny and dry. For those who don't enjoy these elements for the greater part of the year, the temptation is to see the garden as a liability or view its pleasures from the protection of the interior of the house. Ideas for garden living are exemplified in this Australian garden where the house and garden interact, overlap and unite as one living space. Paving, water, seating, planting, canopies and property belong together and create the right atmosphere for outside living. The treatments are simple and harmonious. Brick paving provides a continuous surface throughout, contrasting strongly with the cool blue of the swimming pool. The latter's neat rectilinear hardness works in contrast to the baked-earth colours of brick. Planting is pushed away to form a dark backdrop to the ornamental Lutyens bench. Parasols identify areas for relaxation or eating, shielded from the brilliant sunshine, and dark sun-beds take advantage of a warm corner for occasional sun-bathing.

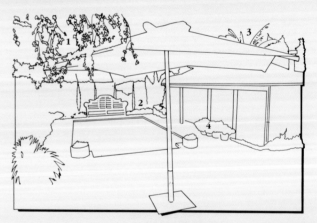

*SCHEME FOR AN AL FRESCO GARDEN*

1 *Betula*
2 *Juniperus scopulorum* "Skyrocket"
3 *Cocos nicifera*
4 Mixed Petunia
5 White Petunia

**Left** *The strong patterns of light and shade contrast with the turquoise pool as a source of bright colour. The umbrella forms a focal point in opposition to the bench and welcomes activity beneath its shade. The bench is for more formal contemplation, the umbrella for informal, spontaneous use.*

**Right** *The heat of the sun is caught in this intimate terrace. Furniture and fencing are given the same wood stain and their dark tints allow the colours of the brickwork to shine in warm red-browns. Planting is pushed back to soften the edges of the paving and one or two terracotta pots introduce bright spots of summer colour.*

**Below right** *The warmth of the brick counters the cool blue water beyond. The change of level sets the pool apart. Whilst it is visible and obviously part of the same garden, the difference in height creates a separation or a physical transition between one area and the other. The contrast in light and shade on these steps is particularly marked; the identification of changes of level in some way is important for reasons of safety.*

**Far left** *The interaction of light, shade and texture here produces a rich, warm and exciting area within the garden. The overhead canopy identifies an area or zone within which pots with decorative bay laurels (*Laurus nobilis*) stand almost like furniture. The lines of paving complement the timber cladding and soft greys, reds and browns work well together.*

# THE OUTDOOR ROOM

By breaking down the boundaries between interior and exterior space, some of the most exciting and stimulating elements of the garden can be put to better use. Planting, sunshine and fragrance can penetrate the interior of the house whilst furniture, music and lighting move outside. A conservatory allows the garden to be enjoyed at close quarters throughout the year but true *al fresco* living really comes into its own in the heat of summer or in the warmer regions of the world. Parasols, awnings, pergolas or screens emphasize or suggest enclosure. Paving patterns or materials can cross the threshold between interior and exterior, and furniture can be chosen so that it is compatible with interior and exterior schemes. Try to retain versatility and freedom in fixtures as built-in barbecues, lighting or seating can be restricting and static. Movable chairs, tables and other fixtures allow you to use an area in a variety of ways, depending on your mood or the weather.

Trees and shrubs can be used to create dappled shade around seating areas – very important in sunny climates. Choose those with light filigree leaves – *Acacia, Acer* or *Robinia*.

*Above The giant umbrella effectively identifies an outdoor room by the extent of its canopy. The walls of the house provide a backdrop and the garden atmosphere infiltrates the open side with planted containers and paving. The colour scheme is palest cream and white, suggesting cool light shade and allowing the planting to dominate with architectural shapes.*

*Left The rectilinear lines of the house are extended into the garden and terrace by this dramatic pergola. This will eventually be softened with plant material to provide further shade and create an extension of the living space, linking the house with the pool. The canopy also identifies a protected area near the house which is sheltered and psychologically safe.*

**Left** *This terrace relies on the simple mixture of whites and creams in paving and painted walls, complemented by the protective umbrella. Foliage and flowers decorate the periphery, and ornamental containers add interest nearer the house.*

**Above** *This terrace is separated from the house, but the paving and the arrangement of the planting suggest enclosure and certainly identify a separate space. The opportunity for dining under the open sky should not be missed.*

# GARDENS FOR CONTEMPLATION

As well as the colour and excitement it offers, one of the greatest values of a garden is that it provides an unrivalled opportunity for relaxation. As a retreat from pressure, noise, frustration or life in general, there is little to surpass it. Quiet corners, shady arbours or seating areas can be arranged or introduced as part of the design to take advantage of particular views, enclosed spaces or sun spots. Pergolas covered in twining climbers can create a special atmosphere of isolation and privacy. The partial canopy overhead creates a barrier through which we can glimpse the sky. Draped with scented flowers, these features become important to sensory perception and make valued hideaways or personal spaces. Gazebos can be used in a similar way.

A simple bench beneath a tree or surrounded by shrub planting may be all that is necessary to create the same effect. Garden swings or hammocks can provide a focus for escapism, underlining the sense of adventure inherent in slipping away. Summerhouses provide useful storage space for furniture and sports equipment perhaps only used in summer. If space allows, these structures become satellite homes where different areas of the garden are suddenly reopened and used, while the main house is vacated.

**FOLIAGE CANOPIES**

To create light canopies of foliage use plant species with fine leaves which allow the sunlight to filter through. Useful trees are *Betula pendula, Robinia pseudacacia,* several of the willows including *Salix × chrysocoma* or *Eucalyptus gunnii.* The traditional cottage garden would have included a large, open apple tree, such as Bramley, under which it is perfect to relax. Climbing plants trained over a pergola or other framework are ideal. The pinnate leaves of *Wisteria sinensis* produce delicate patterns of light and shade. Other climbers can be used singly or in combination to give a succession of blossom. These might include any of the numerous varieties of *Rosa* or *Clematis.* Fragrance adds another dimension and many of the *Rosa* as well as *Jasminum* and the honeysuckles, *Lonicera,* produce a heady perfume. In warmer areas more exotic climbers can be grown such as *Bougainvillea,* adding a vivid splash of colour, or the bright, curiously shaped passion flowers, *Passiflora.* A more formal effect can be achieved with pruned *Pyracantha* or with trained fruit trees.

**Left** *This covered structure creates a focal point in this section of the garden, providing shelter and shade as well as a setting for relaxation and rest. The exotic magenta flowers of* Bougainvillea spectabilis *are beginning to cover the roof while the enormous leaves of* Monstera deliciosa *disguise the roof supports. Eventually the timber frame will be lost from view altogether under rich foliage, producing a dark shady arbour.*

**Above** *The rich blue canopy and pristine white bench look clean and sculptural alongside this decorated swimming pool. The terracotta pot lends a touch of rustic charm against the architectural foliage.*

**Right** *This elegant arbour relies on the thinnest of supports for structure and enclosure, allowing the delicate foliage of the tree canopy to drape outwards and create an informal seating area beneath. The sun filters through to create fine tracery in light and shade on the paving.*

# LEISURE POOLS

Water is a rich source of excitement and colour in any garden and its full enjoyment is important to *al fresco* living. The water feature itself could be a static ornamental reflective pool. Fountains or water cascades introduce dynamic movement and sound, but for sheer fun and *joie de vivre* swimming pools or hot tubs are difficult to beat.

Pools may form a major part of the garden, taking the place of an ornamental lawn. Terraces are relatively easy to combine with the essentially hard contours of swimming pools. Water in the pool can be flush with the paving as long as cut-off drains are incorporated into the terrace. This does away with the sometimes awkward detailing of the pool sides which often emphasizes their artificiality. Although planting may be incorporated in the design fairly close to the pool, the luxurious effect of marginal planting crossing the boundary from land to water cannot.

*Below The darkness of the water in this pool gives it a natural feel in contrast with the more vibrant turquoise or azure blue seen right. It has been achieved by finishing the sides and base of the pool in black lining material. The pool must be made deep enough for diving as the true depth is difficult to gauge; underwater lighting could also help in this respect. The surface of the pool is thus much more reflective, turning it, when not in use, into a large ornamental feature.*

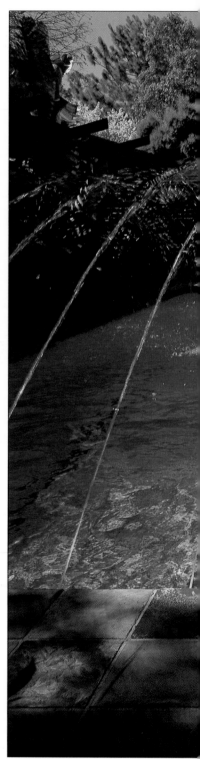

**Above** *Rich planting encloses this private
terrace, the turquoise pool set like a
gemstone into it. The simple circular
shape is emphasized as the important
feature, though the thin lip and upstand
seem functionally awkward. To allow
access all around, the planting has been
set back from the water's edge.*

**Left** *This iridescent pool sparkles with
kingfisher colours and white-water jets,
presenting an irresistible feature. The
neat paving is washed by shadows from
the tropical foliage invading its edge. The
flowing lines are interrupted by a small
promontory which allows the planting to
run almost to the water's edge. The deep
shade and dark green of the planting
contrast with the water jets which disturb
the water surface and introduce both
sound and excitement.*

# TERRACES

The terrace is a valuable asset for outdoor entertaining in the contemporary garden. It should be used as an outside extension of the interior living space complete with furniture, lighting, floor covering and decorative materials and ornamentation. Be as generous as possible with terrace space. It is a functional area for outdoor living and should be capable of containing a table and chairs at least. It also links the house with the garden, becoming an interface or junction between hard, architectural shapes and elevations and soft horizontal planting and lawn areas.

Paving should be simple and hard-wearing and, if pattern is introduced, is best kept strong and bold. Use materials that match or respect the existing materials or that are local or indigenous. Create intimacy with structural planting or arrange planted containers to screen and furnish the space. Introduce colour in the shape of vibrant fabrics for cushions, blinds or screens and use sculpture for drama and focus. Make the terrace a rich and interesting environment and treat it as you would treat your main living room, providing a continuity of design through house and garden.

**Below** *Dry heat is strongly implied in the treatment of this terrace. The baked red-browns of clay tiles and terracotta pots contrast with the clear blue of the sky while the spiny cacti produce stark shadows against the whitewashed walls. The shadows and foliage work strongly together to soften the glare.*

**Left** *The coolness of this shaded terrace is in direct contrast to the one above. The slatted shadows produce geometric patterns, identifying shapes and forms as they fall. The hot tub is a welcome and relaxing addition to even very small terraces, introducing water and a sense of fun in a restricted environment.*

**Right** *This terrace uses weathered timber throughout in contrast to the rich red brick of the house. The decking and furniture look as though they belong together and fit into the site. The hard material is simply detailed and the plant material decorates.*

# COURTYARDS

A courtyard is basically an open space surrounded or enclosed by buildings. Although the predominating features are architectural, the courtyard can be one of the most satisfying and peaceful retreats from the world and the complexities of life, especially when attractive planting is introduced. A courtyard feeling can be created even without a complete enclosure, by screening with plant material or with screens and trellis. Pots, climbers and specimen trees or shrubs are appropriate, often bringing much-needed shade in hot climates. Water is another feature, exploited brilliantly in the Moorish courtyards in Spain. Shade-loving plants may be appropriate as in small enclosed spaces there may be little direct sunlight. Hard paving is the most common surface treatment and walls are frequently whitewashed to increase the feeling of light and space. Overhead screening for seating and entertaining or for relaxation and privacy are important as many courtyards are effectively light wells, overlooked by many windows and balconies.

**Far left** *This bright awning not only affords shade but increases privacy and creates a restricted area. The planting is densely packed to provide a textured screen to protect the privacy of the paved area.*

**Left** *The strong rectilinear lines of this courtyard area have been successfully softened by climbing plants. Hanging baskets introduce bright spots of colour and containers in informally arranged groups break the monotony of paving.*

**Above** *The palm creates bold patterns of light and shade which screen this private area from the glare of the outside world. The simple green, white and terracotta colours are strong and definite, decorated only by texture and shadow.*

# LIGHTING IN THE GARDEN

In a garden used for outdoor living, lighting is an important part of the overall design. Whether functional or decorative, it enables the garden to be appreciated or used well into the night. Although lighting columns can be decorative and sculptural, the garden provides an escape from urban streets and imposed lighting levels. Experiment with the direction and positioning of lighting fixtures. Waist-high lighting bollards provide illumination on a more human scale, lighting pathways, driveways or important routes. Spotlights can direct a beam of light at specific objects and in a similar way uplighters set into the ground will cast curious shadows into the canopies of trees or climbers high above. Wash walls with floodlighting to accentuate architectural details or the textures of brick and stone.

Site plant material to disguise unattractive lighting fixtures and covers during the day and to prevent glare at night. Movable fixtures may be appropriate, usually spotlights on spikes which can be placed into the ground as necessary.

*Above The pool lighting casts an eerie light throughout the swimming pool which is not useful for safe swimming but makes the pool attractive as a garden feature. The spotlighting beyond emphasizes a dramatic planting group, producing strong reflections.*

*Left The terrace is lit by low bollards set into planted borders. The fixtures produce a soft level of light sufficient to identify the pathway. Specimen trees are lit from below for striking shadows and shapes.*

## FORMS OF LIGHTING

A wide variety of exterior light fittings, from decorative fairy lights to spots or floods, are now available. Prominent lighting should be chosen with care. Old or reproduction street lamps have a touch of nostalgia about them but usually look terribly out of place in most gardens, particularly during the daytime. Discreet lighting that vanishes into the background has more to offer. For more specific purposes, cowls or covers may be introduced to deflect or direct light. Lights on permanent display with decorative covers in clear or opalescent glass can be incorporated into the design. Movable lights are available, which need not be left out except when needed and which also have the advantage of being usable in different parts of the garden depending on what you are doing or your mood. For example, it might be possible for a supper party to utilize an area around some fragrant bushes when they are in full flower. Another form of illumination for parties and other events in the garden are flaming torches or flares. These add excitement and moving shadows to the lighting, but great care must be taken with their siting so as to avoid damage to plants.

**Left** *An informal arrangement of lighting spheres on low columns is set into dramatic planting of ferns and palms. Leaf surfaces reflect the glow of light or stand in silhouette against the spheres.*

# THE EDIBLE GARDEN

Fruit and vegetable plots have a utilitarian character that often relegates them to a small patch in the garden at the furthest point from the house. Here, alongside compost heaps, stores of timber and disused machinery, the rows of plants produce their crops. But food production in the garden does not need to be like this. In the wider definition of edible plants all kinds of fruiting, culinary, vegetable and seed-bearing species may be included. Many of these plants are highly decorative and colourful, more than capable of standing alongside more widely accepted flowering or foliage plants.

Even a complete garden could be devoted to edible plants and achieve decorative effect. Many of the more ornate plants are already in common use. The globe artichoke *(Cynara scolymus)* can easily be incorporated into a herbaceous border, as it grows about 1.8m (6ft) tall, with grey-green floral bracts and attractive thistle-like flowers. The heads are edible in the bud stage and the leaves can be used like celery.

Some culinary herbs such as dill *(Peucedanum graveolens)* and fennel *(Foeniculum vulgare)* possess fine feathery leaves and large umbelliferous flowers. Together with angelica *(Angelica archangelica)*, they provide height and foliage interest. Marjoram *(Origanum vulgare)* and thyme *(Thymus vulgaris)* hug the ground with tiny scented leaves while grass-like chives *(Allium schoenoprasum)* give vertical interest in clumps of rich green with the bonus of delicate purple flowers.

Many knot gardens were traditionally devoted to herbs. From medieval times, monasteries would possess a herb garden, usually simply laid out, where the culinary and medicinal plants were grown. In the Renaissance, these gardens became highly elaborate with grand geometric beds, edged with clipped box *(Buxus sempervirens)*, creating formal parterres. Decorative plants and coloured gravels usually filled out the pattern.

Nowadays herbs are usually grown in a much less formal manner, often in free-standing pots. The containers can be arranged in informal groups to take advantage of the sunniest positions or to stand close to the kitchen for easy access when cooking. The idea of low hedging separating plant material can still be applied to the contemporary garden to create controlled colour schemes for borders or terraces. The idea might also be adopted in the vegetable garden to create sections for specific plants. Indeed, the old-fashioned *potager* consisting of formal, neatly arranged beds for herbs and

*By combining flowering plants with fruit and vegetables the functional garden can adopt a decorative character. Flowers may be useful for cutting or simply for infill decoration. The strips of coloured foliage are rich in colour and texture but the vivid splashes of marigold (Tagetes) are most welcome.*

vegetables are still viable today. Some kind of logic and order is required in fruit and vegetable cultivation. From a functional aspect crop rotation, easy access and plot-size are all important considerations when planning a vegetable garden.

### DECORATIVE EDIBLE PLANTS

Each vegetable has an inherent decorative property, whether the tubular vertical leaves of the onion *(Allium cepa)*, the enormous blue-green leaves of cabbage *(Brassica oleracea* "Capitata"*)* or the feathery plumes of carrot *(Daucus carota)*. Use these textures in rows and stripes for strong abstract pattern in a variety of shades from palest green to deepest blue.

Trellis or framework can support beans *(Phaseolus coccineus)* with their decorative orange-red flowers. The frames can be made in a variety of shapes to enclose or screen sections of the garden.

Fruit lends itself to similar training methods with espaliers, fans or cordons tied back to fine wire supports. Their decorative charm is enhanced by delicate blossom in spring and blush-tinted fruits in late summer or early autumn. These growing methods are economical in terms of ground coverage and resultant high cropping, although many free-standing

miniature fruit trees are now available if you prefer.

The protection of a south-facing wall in colder climates can be used to support the fine branches of peaches and nectarines *(Prunus)*. Their downy flesh against the terracotta of old brick or whitewashed surfaces produces a splendid combination of colour and texture. The more alluring charm of the fig *(Ficus carica)* with its decorative and unusual leaf can also be displayed to good effect against a wall, although as a free-standing courtyard specimen it looks even better. Equally attractive are the sinuous branches of the vine *(Vitis vinifera)*, curling out along horizontal supports, garlanded with crenated leaves and blessed with lightly bloomed bunches of purple or green-white grapes. Many of the vine species are used as decorative plants regardless of their fruiting capacity, which comes as an added bonus. Their large leaves are handsome and colour extremely well in autumn.

Soft fruits such as blackberry *(Rubus fruticosus)*, raspberry *(Rubus idæus)* and strawberry *(Fragaria × ananassa)* can also cross the divide between decorative and functional plants. Their rich and luscious fruits complement their delicate flowers or arching forms. In the traditional cottage garden the edible plants were mixed among flowers and shrubs. The informality of those working gardens is a much sought-after style, far removed from the efficient but sterile contemporary fruit and vegetable garden.

Ground-covering plants such as strawberry and marjoram would grow together with carrots or peas *(Pisum sativum)*, sprinked in between with flowering plants such as delphinium *(Delphinium consolida)*, lupin *(Lupinus polyphyllus)* and hollyhock *(Althaea rosea)*. The primose *(Primula vulgaris)*, heartsease *(Viola tricolor)* and daffodil *(Narcissus pseudonarcissus)* would also decorate the garden. Flowers rich in nectar would be included to feed the bees to produce honey.

Many of the idyllic scenes of cottage gardens can be reproduced in the contemporary garden with improved varieties and more colourful species. Vivid purple or russet-fringed cabbages, such as "Sekito", an ornamental variety, or "Ruby Red", can decorate the border, surrounded by decorative herbs such as bronze fennel *(Foeniculcum vulgare* "Giant Bronze"*)*, purple sage *(Salvia officinalis* "Purpurascens"*)* or the silver curry plant *(Helichrysum angustifolium)*.

These combinations of edible species interplanted with delicate roses, herbs and soft fruits are the true prizes of the edible garden, providing treats for the eye as well as the palate.

In planning for produce, take time to consider your requirements. Think of the edible species as alternative options to the standard range of flowering plants or decorative shrubs. They possess similar textural foliage or colour properties. Many are compatible with most other garden plants, and have the extra qualities that excite our taste buds and decorate our plates. Little in life is quite as fulfilling, or tastes quite as good, as growing your own.

**Below** *Rows of different vegetables produce stripes of textured green, like some abstract painting or collage. This kind of decoration is incidental to the production of crops which demands neatness and order, but in a large kitchen garden, for instance, the effect can be very dramatic.*

**Right** *This simple herb garden uses the plants around the main entrance. The sunny location will produce strong scents and vigorous growth. Incorporate the herbs in pots too, which may be arranged or rearranged at will. Herbs such as thyme (Thymus), mint (Mentha) or chamomile (Anthemis) may be introduced to invade paved areas, softening the harsh lines and filling cracks with foliage.*

**Left** *This recreation of a cottage garden mixes herbs, vegetables, fruit and flowers in decorative combinations. As a working garden, many would prefer a more ordered approach which can look sterile in comparison, but many combinations of these plants are possible.*

## VEGETABLE GARDEN AT VILLANDRY, FRANCE

The vegetable garden at Villandry is a masterpiece of formal ornamental design using plant material that is rarely treated in this way. A huge area of terrace is devoted to intricate patterns and colours where gravel walkways form a backdrop, with low clipped hedges of box *(Buxus sempervirens)* retaining any unruly material. Colour is provided by foliage, though standard roses create bright splashes of red or pink at important junctions.

The garden is vast and contains a huge variety of crops – some ornamental, some edible. The fresh green foliage of young transplanted crops of lettuce or carrots contrasts with the rich purple or blue-green leaves of ornamental cabbage, artichoke or broccoli. The whole layout was designed to be viewed from a high terrace to do full justice to its intricacy and rich variety of textures. The seasonal variations implicit in a system using crop rotation make this a complex and high-maintenance style of garden which requires a great deal of pre-planning and organization. Although Villandry is too massive to be copied in its entirety, the individual components could be re-created in relatively small kitchen gardens, and work well as showpieces of design rather than humble vegetable plots.

**Left** *The maze-like geometry of these planting beds is accentuated by the neatly trimmed box hedging (Buxus sempervirens). Individually, the standard roses look rather lost but when the whole garden is seen their delicate heads of strong flower colour float above the rich mosaic of the vegetable beds.*

**Above** *The dramatic heads of ornamental cabbage (Brassica oleracea "Capitata") produce cactus-like shapes to form the main elements of this decorative pattern. Their regimented rows dissect the larger square to enable other decorative beds to provide colour or texture between.*

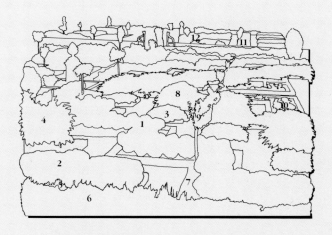

## SCHEME FOR A VEGETABLE GARDEN

*1* Ornamental cabbage
*2* Ornamental kale
*3* Spinach
*4* Jerusalem artichoke
*5* Rudbeckia
*6* Salvia farinacea "Victoria"

*7* Buxus sempervirens "Suffruticosa"
*8* Cardoon
*9* Standard rose
*10* Strawberries
*11* Leeks
*12* Sweet corn/maize

**Right** *The fresh greens of newly planted vegetables run in straight rows between the hedges, creating strips of colour against the weed-free soil. Vibrant bedding colours beyond produce a rich contrast and welcome relief from the all-pervasive green, while roses provide decoration above.*

# THE FRUIT GARDEN

Fruit in the garden can provide unexpected visual delights. Shining apples with russet streaks bring colour to the orchard, or even to a single tree if space is limited while green pears dangle from dark branches.

These fruits can be grown as dwarf pyramids or more decoratively as fans, cordons or espaliers trained along fine wires or against a warm protective wall. Soft fruits such as the blushing velvety peach *(Prunus persica)* or the smooth-skinned nectarine can be grown in the same way. As they will not bear fruit without protection, they need a south- or west-facing wall. The early blossom is prone to damage by spring frosts and in some areas will need the protection of glass. More hardy fruits, such as gooseberry *(Grossularia uva-crispa)* or raspberry *(Rubus idaeus)*, can do without this protection and will form decorative arching or densely-packed shrubs. Their soft delicate fruits hide beneath protective leaves but if you intend to harvest your crop you would be wise to cover the bushes with netting. Strawberries *(Fragaria × ananassa)* can produce quite decorative ground-cover with delicate white flowers and extensive runners. More exotic fruits need the protection of glass in colder climates but in tropical zones the enormous leaves of *Musa* (banana) can be used for their glorious foliage.

**Left** *The glowing green fruits of quince* (Cydonia oblonga) *are displayed to effect against the decorative brick wall. The wall not only affords protection but provides a backdrop of colour and geometric shape.*

**Above** *The light pergola frame displays* Citrus limon *at its best – as a decorative plant with attractive scented fruits. The permeating light decorates the foliage and provides dappled shade beneath. The elliptic evergreen leaves are highly ornamental and the red-tinged flowers, earlier in the season, are strongly scented.*

*Right* Tucked into a sheltered corner in the vegetable patch this terracotta pot is purpose-made for strawberry-growing. Small openings in the sides allow young plants to be grown all around the pot as well as from the top. The result is a mass of leaf and flower followed by a rich crop of scarlet strawberries, ideal for a patio or backyard, where their decorative effect alone would make them welcome.

*Above* These trusses of redcurrant, (Ribes), almost hidden by decorative leaves, produce a rich wine-red mass of shiny berries. Grown here against the rigid geometry of a supporting frame, the garlands of leaves and fruit look sumptuous enough for a Bacchanalian feast.

# HERB GARDEN

Herbs have been a part of garden design for thousands of years, cultivated for medicinal, culinary or purely decorative reasons. Their charm lies in their appearance but also in the knowledge that this disparate range of plants has other physical properties of flavour, scent, medication or preservation. They may be massed according to their decorative appearance as dense ground-cover, low shrubs, tall elegant plants or coloured foliage specimens or masses. Originally their appearance was secondary to their use and planting plans can still be arranged as functional working borders.

The art of a good herb garden is in managing to organize the plant material with both function and aesthetics in mind. Trends in more adventurous home-cooking and entertaining have ensured that many of the more popular herbs at least will have a place in many gardens. Herbs are often grown alongside other decorative plants in sunny borders or, more commonly, in pots or containers which should be grouped for decorative effect. Sections of the garden may be devoted to one or two herbs in particular. The chamomile lawn using *Anthemis nobilis* is an effective use of ground-cover which produces scent when bruised or crushed.

***Above*** *This simple terracotta pot is crammed with herbs for a textured arrangement in miniature. The large leaves of* Rumex acetosa *are sprinkled with the more delicate forms of* Foeniculum, Lavandula, Allium *and* Mentha. Tropaeolum majus *skirts the base of the pot.*

***Left*** *The tall spikes of* Oenothera *and* Verbascum *dominate this border with lemon-yellow flowers. Beneath,* Origanum *and* Thymus *form a dense carpet of ground-cover, stealing colour from the surrounding plants.*

**Left** *The qualities of* Allium schoenoprasum *as a ground-covering plant are rarely used. Its fine texture in deep blue-green complements the delicate purple heads. Here used in conjunction with* Allium afflatunense *the similarities are underlined by the difference in size. Alliums possess some fine decorative flower heads which can reach 10-12cm (4-5in) across and a height of 1.2m (4ft) or more.*

# THE POTAGER

The French word *potager* is used to describe a formally arranged garden devoted as much to herbs as flowers. Generally, edible plants are included more for decoration than for culinary use. Many designs were highly complicated and ornamental – not dissimilar to the grand parterre. Most culinary or edible plants do not possess a strong shape or bold structure and so, by arranging plants together in restricted shapes or planting beds, a stronger decorative effect could be achieved than by using them individually.

Colour co-ordination is important. Herbs can be arranged for foliage colour in the same way as you would plan a flower border. Blue-greens, dark greens, silver-grey or yellow leaf colours are prevalent in herb species. Purple cabbages can provide highlights of strong deep colour and

*Foeniculum vulgare* "Giant Bronze", as its name suggests, projects feathered bronze fronds high into the air. Herbs themselves are often used as hedging to frame the complex shapes. *Lavandula, Helichrysum, Hyssopus, Teucrium* and *Thymus* may all be used for hedging or edging. *Santolina chamaecyparissus* makes a bold silver-white splash of colour and is strongly scented. *Santolina virens* gives a feathery green in contrast. The hedging species would be clipped into formal shapes in a similar way that *Buxus* is in the parterre or knot garden. Use colour and texture within these shapes to create a formal pattern that is ideally viewed from above for best effect. Try to use seasonal variations in leaf colour and rotate crops to give interest throughout the year.

# THE ORIENTAL GARDEN

Oriental gardens are envisaged as the natural landscape in miniature. In the philosophies of Zen Buddhism and Shinto in Japan, and Taoism in China, the elements of the landscape (of which man is seen as an integral part) are worshipped or revered, endowed with energy, harmony and beauty.

In China the "yang", or male force, is personified in rocks, hills or mountains whilst the "yin", or female force, is embodied in the softness of water. In Japan, Zen Buddhism concentrates the mind on the landscape in order to divine a meaning to life itself.

The symbolism evident in the gardens of both countries is inscrutable and difficult to understand outside the religious or secular philosophies involved but this in no way affects our appreciation of their style and elegance, even though a true re-creation of the oriental garden outside China or Japan is impossible.

## BASIC PRINCIPLES

Balance in art and design is essential in the oriental garden, though not achieved through the symmetry or formality accepted in the West. Opposites such as light and shade, and vertical and horizontal emphases are offset against each other. The contemplation of these forms and harmonies is at the very heart of this garden style where the aim is to create a haven of peace and tranquillity in which nature restores the inner being.

The garden is often seen as part of the house, blurring the distinction between indoors and outdoors. The house platform continues into the garden space, devoid of balustrades, handrails and other barriers. Screens are often used to demarcate the interior space, which can be opened up to bring the garden into the house.

A sense of space is an important element in the oriental garden. The landscape in microcosm should have no easily identifiable boundaries. Perspective is manipulated by the juxtaposition of large-scale elements in the foreground with small-scale background scenery, and the peripheries of the garden planted densely to absorb winding pathways, hiding their destination. Elements from adjoining gardens or landscapes are purposely integrated into the design to give the illusion of scale.

The Zen Buddhist gardens in rock and gravel are even more carefully considered as an allegorical model of man's journey to eternity. These

*This Western interpretation of Japanese style includes the essential features of the oriental garden. The textured surfaces, weathered stone and contorted branches of Acer palmatum "Dissectum" are full of unusual intrigue. Shaded beneath the planting is a bamboo deer-scarer.*

*Left The oriental style of garden design is ideal for restricted space. By using materials sparingly the concept of space is increased. Plant material and hard surfaces are balanced and textural. Ornament is kept to a minimum and the materials themselves are allowed to decorate. Timber is contrasted with carefully chosen rocks, and fine-textured ground-covers and low shrubs counteract the architectural forms of the ferns.*

*Below left The white gravel surface brings light into this dark corner, broken by irregular slabs like stepping stones. The fine texture of the gravel is repeated in the tiny-leaved ground-cover,* Helxine soleirolii, *which acts as a bright foil to bold dark-leaved plants. The foliage plants of* Prunus laurocerasus *"Otto Luyken",* Aucuba japonica *and* Acer palmatum *build up a backdrop of colour and texture alongside the pattern of bamboo fencing. Water drops from the hollow deer-scarer to form a shallow pool, floating a reflective surface above the gravel paving. Texture is important in the oriental garden, where foliage shape and pattern rather than flowers are used to create interest.*

gardens are intended for uplifting contemplation. Carefully chosen rocks are set into raked gravel, with simple mounds of moss offering a hint of green.

The spirituality and symbolism inherent in the oriental garden makes it hard to copy. Other factors such as climate, soils and vegetation particular to China and Japan make the task yet more difficult. The idea that a smattering of miniature pagodas, lanterns or bamboo pipes will make a successful oriental garden should be discounted immediately. Yet some of the philosophy behind these gardens can be understood and developed to provide an alternative outside the Far East.

"Less is more" is a concept associated with the Minimalist movement in fine art. That same principle is echoed in oriental garden design. Colour schemes are often subdued or monochromatic, flowers are restricted, blossom trees used as individual specimens or asymmetric arrangements of boulders are balanced against smooth reflective sheets of water or textured gravel beds.

The spatial qualities resulting from omitting material are far more relevant that the mass of detail, colour or form associated with many Western gardens. By choosing individual plants or grouping interesting speciments together in well-balanced combinations set against a neutral backdrop or surface, attention is drawn to the qualities of those particular species. Similarly the simplicity of the textured gravel beds complements winding pathways or stepping stones, moss-covered islands or symbolic rocks, before slipping beneath shallow pools of water to create shimmering patterns of light and reflection.

## PLANT MATERIAL

The flowering cherry, quince or azalea immediately conjure up a picture of Japan. Mixed together for spring effect in Western gardens, these free-flowering species can appear gaudy and brash. Although these plants are used in the oriental gardens they are put to much use often singly. Large maples, usually thinned, or contorted pines may be positioned closer to the house or viewing platform through which much smaller-leaved species, such as azalea or bamboo are glimpsed.

For selected or specimen plants choose the delicate Japanese maple *(Acer palmatum),* Yoshino cherry *(Prunus* "Yoshino"*)* or camellia. The latter two may be chosen for their exquisite flower, the former for its intense autumn hues. The fine grassy texture of bamboo is useful as a foil to gravel or stone and can also be used in its ground-covering varieties.

The borders of the garden are usually lost in dark evergreens which also serves as a backdrop to important plants. *Cryptomeria* may be used together with *Camellia, Photinia* or possibly *Rhododendron.*

Stones are chosen for their individual spiritual significance, though certain shapes are common. For example, tall vertical shapes symbolize the body, whilst short verticals symbolize the soul. The mind and body together are embodied in a horizontal stone.

The individual pieces can symbolize features in the landscape and arching or reclining stones are greatly prized for these elements. Their patina is important, showing age and weathering and muted grey- and buff-coloured forms are most favoured.

## GROUPING HARD MATERIALS

Stones should be grouped in odd numbers at important points within the garden or to create a focal point. Moss, gravel or shingles can be used to create a setting for the stones which is most dramatically exemplified in the dry garden, or "kare-sansui". Here the gravel should be as fine as possible so that it can be raked into elaborate patterns. A wide-gapped wooden rake is normally used to create ripple patterns, symbolic of water.

Water itself is also seen as symbolic, in contrast to the stone elements. It is used in a range of sizes, from tiny pools in stone basins (chozu-bachi), associated with cleansing rituals in the tea gardens of Japan, to light-reflecting shallow wide streams or lakes. Rocks and boulders may edge these pools, the spaces between filled with moss, lichen or gravel.

*Left This garden is influenced by oriental style and uses bold foliage effects contrasted with textural gravel and pebbles. The planting is dense enough to hide the boundaries of this relatively small space, leaving glimpses of area or activity beyond. The* Alchemilla mollis *forms a decorative foil to the more dynamic foliage of* Yucca *and* Miscanthus.

*Right The rich texture of lichen-covered rock is warmed by evening sun, depicting intricate patterns contrasting with the cool water beyond. The shiny green leaf of* Eichhornia *squeezes through the crevice.*

## ORIENTAL TOWN GARDEN, BARNES, LONDON

The influence of Japanese style on this town garden is unmistakable. Foliage planting is strong and manages to disguise the true size of the garden very well. The paving is textured by small cobbles either set together in a mortar bed or loose-laid with rectangular stepping stones leading towards the pool and seating area beyond. Dark timber decking associates well with the water features giving a contemporary character that is still in keeping with the Japanese tradition. Bamboo hurdles are used to screen out any unwanted materials such as brick, which are obviously Western. The planting is dense but structural, using architectural foliage and forms well to unify the different areas of the garden. If space allowed, a slightly more spartan scheme would be possible, allowing individual plants or groups of plants to act as specimens. Free-standing material could then be viewed from every angle whilst the space between the plants creates depth and interest. Flowers are of secondary interest in this style of garden apart, perhaps, from a solitary flowering cherry or camellia. The planting groups effectively divide the space so that the terracing or decking around the pool is hidden from the further end of the garden, while a simple bridge joining the two areas creates a transitional element. The incorporation of garden furniture, and even a hot-tub, has been treated sufficiently sympathetically not to detract from the customary simplicity of Japanese design.

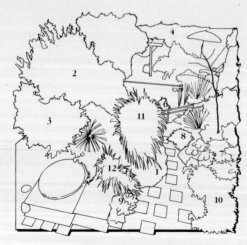

### SCHEME FOR AN ORIENTAL GARDEN

*1 Alchemilla mollis*
*2 Philadelphus*
*3 Ligustrum ovalifolium*
  *"Aureum"*
*4 Vitis coignetiae*
*5 Betula*
*6 Sagittaria sagittifolia*

*7 Arundinaria*
*8 Hosta*
*9 Sedum*
*10 Prunus*
*11 Miscanthus*
*12 Yucca*

*Left* The foliage planting provides a wealth of textures, shapes and forms that interrupt the view through the garden. There are tantalizing glimpses of unexpected elements, such as the yellow parasol or the hammock. The route into the area beyond is purposely indirect, using the full width of the garden to give an illusion of space.

*Left* The design of this typical rectangular urban plot cleverly conceals its true dimensions by dividing the area into quite distinct compartments. These have been successfully unified by the large groups of architectural foliage plants and the repetition of hard-surfacing material.

*Above* In the decked area unusual pots filled with foliage plants provide ornamentation, as do the cushions which create an informal seating area. The reflective surface of the pool disappears beneath the deck, the dark shade cleverly disguising the technique of construction.

# SURFACE TREATMENTS

Surface treatment in oriental gardens is of prime importance. In the Zen gardens the raked gravel symbolizing water is luminous, textured and rippled, surrounding the carefully arranged and symbolic rocks. The gravel is not a functional surface to be trodden but a sculpted layer to be contemplated and admired. The texture of gravels, pebbles and boulders run through Chinese and Japanese gardens complementing plant material, stone slabs and water. Stone or timber stepping stones usually meander artfully through the garden, often set into finer gravels. They were originally used in tea ceremonies to prevent guests muddying their feet. They serve now to slow the pace as one moves through the garden. Timber or large flat slabs of stone may also be used for simple bridges over streams or pools; water is used for stillness and its reflective properties, contrasted with more textured material.

**Far left** *The decorative textures of the foliage reflect light against dark green shade. Contrasted against the matt surfaces of river, stone and mottled gravel, the combinations work well. The neutral tones of the garden wall recede behind the planting and the foreground is consequently emphasized.*

**Left** *The reflective surface of water is complemented by the lustrous surface of the slate. The muted tones of blue and dark grey are lit by the emerald green of water hyacinth (Eichhornia crassipes). The rectangular slabs appear to float or hover on the surface of the water as no means of support are visible. The effect is elegant and controlled.*

**Above** *The rocks of temple or monastery gardens are allegorical symbols of man's passage through the world. They are set into a sea of gravel, carefully and purposefully raked to be contemplated and considered. These surfaces and forms are open to individual interpretation, to be seen and admired from a distance – a high art form of Zen Buddhism.*

# ORNAMENT

Ornament in the oriental garden is not considered essential as the planting, rocks and gravel are imbued with all the necessary decoration, texture and character. If ornaments are to be used, exercise restraint and don't over-decorate – they were of religious importance and were never used merely for ornament. Lanterns should be used only to shed light, perhaps over a pathway, stepping stones or bridge. They may be employed as a focal point in an arrangement of bamboos, grasses or moss. Made of stone, they were originally used in Korea, but were taken up and modified by the Japanese to suit their own gardens. Candlelight is the usual form of illumination and may be used in smaller lanterns suspended from trees or vertical supports. Stone basins used in the Tea Ceremony may be large boulders with a rough-hewn hollow to collect water or they be more formally shaped and carved. Hollow bamboo pipes feed the water into the pool where it is used for washing or cleansing. Deer-scarers are also made of bamboo, and operate by water dripping from a high pipe into a lower pipe which is pivoted. The lower pipe fills with water and becoming top-heavy tips to splash the water out into a pool. The pipe swings back, hitting a stone and emitting an echoing sound, thus scaring the deer.

**Left** *The stone basin* (chozu-bachi) *is smoothly rounded to support the water and bamboo ladle. The colours are strong and atmospheric, suggestive of damp mossy shade. Overflowing water would soak away below the container and the ground would be covered by pebbles or gravel.*

**Below** *This Buddha sits rather begrudgingly on a simple granite slab. Originally intended as a shrine perhaps, the sculpture is also decorative. The simple backdrop of greenery and stone emphasizes the stylistic decoration of the idol.*

**Right** *This carved basin shelters below* Azalea *and* Acer palmatum, *reflecting the tracery of their branches. The basin sits on a pebble-strewn surface to prevent the surrounding soil becoming waterlogged or muddy and to decorate. Moss completes the arrangement, complementing the green foliage above. The flowers introduce colour to an otherwise restrained scheme.*

# ARCHITECTURAL PLANTING

The form, shape and texture of planting in the oriental garden are of prime importance. Specimens and plant associations are studied structurally and meticulously arranged. Often the softness of plant material is balanced against textural surfaces such as fine gravel or against the bold massive solidity of carefully chosen and placed rocks. Architectural planting in the West is usually associated with striking, large foliage. In the East, the architecture is discovered in delicate stem patterns, incised leaves, decorative shape and contorted or dynamic forms. Rather than massing plants together to create structure and density the structure of the plant material itself articulates a message, perhaps of strength and energy, or of softness and gentle quietness. The intricate patterns of *Acer palmatum* bending low over gravel beds and mossy rocks is typical of this genre.

*Below These carefully pruned shapes of box* (Buxus sempervirens) *possess the strength and density of stone, yet are soft, textured and restfully green. The informally arranged group is massed around a pathway, producing a focal point which also draws attention to the adjacent water feature.*

132

**Left** *The power of these massive boulders is softened and complemented by the delicate stem tracery above and the pebbles below. The play of light is also decorative.*

**Above** *The luxuriant foliage of Hosta counters the hard decoration of pebbles covering the ground. The hot red growths of Photinia contrast again but do not succeed as well against the pale lilac spires of the Hosta flowers.*

# SCREENS AND SURROUNDS

As space is often restricted in Japanese gardens the boundaries are usually hidden by foliage plants, which obliterate or obscure the true size of the garden. Where this is not possible, decorative screens are used to maintain privacy or distract the eye. Bamboo is the most commonly used material, though timber, usually stained, is also used. Decorative open lattice-work fences allow glimpses of the landscape beyond the garden whilst still identifying the boundary.

Traditionally the bamboo was held together by twine, though nowadays the knots and fastenings are a purely decorative device to disguise nails or pins. Other fences are erected as frames with the bamboo held tightly packed within. Of much more solid construction, they provide a visual barrier, stopping views and vistas with textured density.

Screening may also play a part in furnishing or decorating the junction between the house and garden, closing together to shut out the garden or opening to enlarge the living space by combining the interior and exterior parts of the property. In creating an oriental-style garden in the West, these textured screens may be attached to boundary walls to disguise the brick or stone work which would jar as a foreign material. If you stain timber supports black or dark brown, they will contrast attractively with the yellow-browns of the bamboo.

*Right* This Japanese-style garden relies heavily on the screening potential of bamboo to disguise the enclosing walls. This does not suggest space beyond, but simply applies a texture more sympathetic to the designer's aims. The timbers are suggestive of screens, stained black against a white background. Colour within the garden is restrained and subdued – foliage greens, timber browns and the dark grey of stone. The water, almost black from the reflected shadow, reads as a contrasting colour, and the paving treatment is simple and directional, while the timber decking appears to float above the textured garden, like an overlay of harmonious material pulled back to reveal decoration beneath. Ornament is restricted to one stone lantern – the stones and plant material are decorative enough.

**Top** *This Tokyo fence illustrates the rich colour combination of tawny bamboo against dark timber. The contrast is strengthened by the dark green and brown landscape beyond which is an important element in the whole scene. The fence is bold and decorative yet functions more as a visual screen than a physical barrier. The criss-cross pattern is typical of traditional Japanese fencing.*

**Above** *This imposing fence presents a much more formidable barrier, and is concerned more with privacy, shelter and impenetrability. Tantalizing glimpses of the garden beyond are allowed through the gate timbers and the textured screens allow light and some plant material to squeeze through. The entrance is emphasized by a change of material and colour, and by the decorative lintel.*

# THE FLOWER GARDEN

Flowers are at the forefront of most gardeners' minds. Perhaps it is their purity of colour which attracts us, their abstract simplicity or their impressionistic sweeps of colour seen from a distance, catching the eye or presenting an image of romantic charm. In seeking to capture these snap-shots of nature in our gardens, we sometimes lose the freshness and naive charm of nature's creations and substitute them with gaudy, ostentatious alternatives.

Ideally, you should use flowers as sparingly or carefully as you would use decoration in your home. Too much information in pattern, colour and shape can lead to a tangled, incoherent mess. Value flowers, treasure their specific qualities and set them like jewels in a frame, contrasted with neutral foliage to enhance and accentuate their worth.

## COLOUR

Flower colour can be manipulated by the gardener to produce co-ordinated, sophisticated colour schemes, mixing colours within a range to provide harmonious sweeps from white to pink, pink to red, red to orange and so on. Alternatively, a single colour may be adopted as a theme where flowers are restricted to monochromatic white, quiet pastels or hot oranges and yellows.

Gertrude Jekyll and Vita Sackville-West both brought this style to perfection.

Alternatively, use strength of flower colour to produce abstract shapes or masses in fiery red, brilliant yellow or vivid blue. Foliage helps to emphasize shape or provide atmosphere with spires of cordyline (*Cordyline australis*), Yucca (*Yucca gloriosa*) or bamboo (*Arundinaria japonica*).

Colour-themed garden borders are difficult to achieve and require a great deal of planning. Whilst a number of different flowers may sit happily within a colour range, the various species used may not flower in the sequence intended; equally they may all flower at once. Foliage characteristics then play a more important role, and have little in common with the intended scheme.

It takes careful planning and a great deal of trial and error to achieve anything like perfection. Gertrude Jekyll was renowned for her schematic border planting detailed in her book, *Colour Schemes for the Flower Garden*, and her early artistic training certainly helped her. Painterly inspiration is also evident in Monet's gardens at Giverny, which show control of flower colour combinations inspired by the painter's experience.

It is important to understand about colour harmonies and contrasts. Contrasting colours are opposites in the spectrum, so red opposes green and

*The flower heads of* Lilium regale, Allium giganteum *and* Verbascum olympicum *all share a certain light-reflecting quality. The sulphur-yellow and rich purple of* Verbascum *and* Allium *respectively are echoed in the huge trumpet-like flowers of* Lilium, *which blows its powerful scent around the garden.*

garden may be hungering for a group of white lilies or for something of the palest lemon yellow, but it is not allowed to have it because it is a blue garden ... my own idea is that it should be beautiful first and then just as blue as may be expected with its best possible beauty."

## SCENTED FLOWERS

Scent is often inseparable from flower although many foliage plants may release their own, usually when bruised or crushed. A flower's perfume is released without coaxing, floating freely across the air to excite our senses. There can be few more evocative experiences than the triggering of a memory by a smell or fragrance, transporting us back to some long-forgotten experience in an instant.

Spring flowers have a curious sweetness of their own, a little cloying but a welcome harbinger of the feast awaiting us in summer. Other early perfumes are released from Chinese witch-hazel *(Hamamelis mollis)*, mahonia *(Mahonia japonica)* and magnolia *(Magnolia × soulangiana)*.

Summer wafts in the strong scents of lavender *(Lavandula spica* "Hidcote"*)*, lily *(Lilium regale)*, honeysuckle *(Lonicera periclymenum)*, wisteria *(Wisteria sinensis)*, tobacco plant *(Nicotiana*, various forms*)*, mock orange *(Philadelphus coronarius)* and myrtle *(Myrtus communis)*. These much sweeter scents should be used sparingly. A single fragrance will last in the memory and will be appreciated all the more without competition.

## DECORATIVE FLOWER FORMS

We appreciate flowers particularly for their decorative qualities. Their intricate patterns and exquisite forms express purity, perfection and beauty.

Highly structured flowers, such as lily *(Lilium)*, day lily *(Hemerocallis)*, rose *(Rosa)* and paeony *(Paeonia)* are feats of architectural design in miniature. They possess exotic qualities and compete successfully with even the fabulous tropical species such as passion flower *(Passiflora caerulea)* and bird of paradise *(Strelitzia reginae)*.

More simple arrangements of petals, usually single flowers, are often overlooked as horticulturalists seek ever more decorative flowers. The purity and simplicity of the Himalayan blue poppy *(Meconopsis betonicifolia)*, tree mallow *(Lavatera arborea)*, quince *(Chaenomeles speciosa* or *C. × superba)* and camellia are valuable additions to many borders.

Some trees produce quite stunning flowers, apart from the heavy pink clusters of the much-favoured flowering cherry. The tulip tree *(Liriodendron tulipifera)*, famed for its unusual leaf, is covered in yellow-green flowers in high summer. Cream candlestick flowers stand erect all over the horse chestnut *(Aesculus hippocastanum)* in late spring and its graceful, drooping white bracts give *Davidia involucrata* its common names of pocket handkerchief tree or dove tree.

yellow opposes purple. To achieve harmony, these opposites need to balance each other within a particular colour scheme.

Pastel colours tinted with white achieve a harmonious range more easily. Few colour clashes or contrasts are possible within this range as the purity and strength are absent. The proportions or amounts of colour used may also achieve a kind of harmony or balance. When organizing a colour theme border it is important to remember that warmer colours such as reds, oranges and yellows appear to advance towards you and appear closer than blues, greens and violets, which tend to recede into the distance.

If planning a single-colour-themed border, do not exclude all other colours. A white garden can include other tones, perhaps yellow and certainly green in small amounts. In the words of Gertrude Jekyll, "a blue

The golden rain of laburnum (*Laburnum* × *watereri* "Vossii") brings sunlit yellow into the garden with its long drooping racemes of flowers. It is possible to train laburnum against a wall or over a pergola or archway.

Trees or large flowering shrubs should be used to introduce structure to the flowering border. They have a mass and solidity which holds together the often disparate shapes of flowering plants.

As an alternative backdrop use climbers such as wisteria (*Wisteria sinensis*), clematis (*Clematis*), rose (*Rosa*), climbing hydrangea (*Hydrangea petiolaris*) and canary creeper (*Tropaeolum peregrinum*).

Unusual flowers should be used sparingly to avoid the curiosity factor. It pays to think of flowering plants as the essential fabric of the garden rather than a collection of ornaments. One or two exotic specimens among more mundane species will add to their effect and increase their value.

*Fatsia japonica* produces globular bream-green umbels to match the summer heads of angelica (*Angelica archangelica*). Verbascum spires flash with sulphurous yellow flowers almost hidden in grey woolly leaves, tiny gypsophila flowers (*Gypsophila paniculata*) float cloud-like amongst the undergrowth and feathery astilbe or rodgersia complement it with pinks and creamy whites. Schizophragma (*Schizophragma integrifolia*) suspends graceful teardrops from its climbing branches whilst below the elegant arum lily (*Zantedeschia aethiopica*) is difficult to surpass.

Enjoy the design possibilities presented by flower gardening. The cottage garden look may be regarded as a relatively easy option where wonderful combinations of flowers are the result of happy accident. The cottage garden, often perceived as the epitome of the flower garden also contained fruit and vegetables as it had to be functional.

*Left* *This narrow pathway is almost hidden by overhanging borders of flower. The hot pinks of roses and scarlets of poppies are balanced by the cooler white of* Chrysanthemum *and the tall spikes of pale pink foxgloves* (Digitalis). *The path could be a little wider to match the line of the steps though some of the overgrown charm would be lost.*

*Right* *The rose garden is one of the most popular images of flower gardening and certainly the profusion and quality of flower of any rose is difficult to match. Display the flowers against dark foliage backgrounds for the best contrast. This also helps to disguise the awkward shape of the shrubs, which often become leggy or disfigured by pruning. Using ground-cover beneath the plants is another option. Grow roses for scent and colour, rather than as a horticultural exercise which often results in patchy colour from individual plants or flowers.*

## MONET'S GARDEN AT GIVERNY, FRANCE

The planting in Monet's garden at Giverny is a particularly good source of inspiration for using flowers within a garden. The stronger colours of flowers need control and careful mixing even when the intention is to startle with a brilliant display. In this garden, seasonal planting for strong colours and more subtle flowering shrubs have been combined with spectacular success and the famous lily pond makes a graceful, quiet oasis of textured greenery and reflective water.

In a celebration of colour in this famous garden, flowers have been grouped in broad masses and sweeps to brilliant effect. When planning a flower border, it is important to think of flowers not as individual blooms but rather as a coloured surface or form which can be combined within a broad colour range or used *en masse* for simple abstract shape and hue.

Use shrubs and trees for a framework, and float pools of colour between or beneath. Once a broad impression has been achieved with flowers, drop in some bright contrasts. Colour can be manipulated, strengthened, weakened, complemented or contrasted. If flowers are to be the major element in the planting, restrict the use of decorative foliage. Keep neutral hedging trimmed to a uniform surface, as a backcloth for rich flower patterns. Make use of shade from trees and shrubs to focus attention on yellow and white flowers which may shine out from it. Use reds for brightness and warmth or blue for coolness and mystery. Above all, experiment with colour and enjoy the spectacular results.

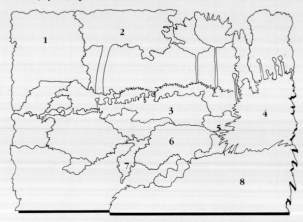

### SCHEME FOR A FLOWER GARDEN

*1 Rosa*
*2 Malus*
*3 Tulipa* (Darwin hybrids)
*4 Papaver orientale*
*5 Arabis caucasica*
*6 Paeonia lactiflora*
*7 Cheiranthus cheirii*
*8 Hemerocallis*

**Left** Achillea filipendula *and* Rudbeckia hirta *vie for sunlit positions, producing glowing reflective yellow against a rich green backdrop. Their heights and flowering periods are well matched, making them a memorable combination in late summer. The timing of flower production is particularly important in colour schemes.*

**Right** Impatiens walleriana *in the foreground and the zonal pelargoniums behind compete to produce the brightest red. Against the green foliage, red is very strong and the odd pink flower in the pelargonium bed actually makes the red brighter and warmer although these two colours do not mix well in large groups.*

**Left** *Tulips are quite difficult flowers to use as their large cups of colour are too vivid and rich against the fresher shades of spring. But despite the colour balances here, there is a strong impressionist feel to the vibrant dots of colour floating against a background of softer greens and pinks.*

**Above** *The bare arches of the pergola allow enough sunshine through to wash the gravel beneath in bright light.* Tropaeolum majus *takes advantage and clothes the floor in a carpet of shining leaves and orange-yellow flowers. The intensity of colour is increased by the rich reds and purples of* Aster novi-belgii *and* Dahlia.

# THE SCENTED GARDEN

Scent is a powerful and evocative element in garden design which is difficult to control and quantify. Not all scents are pleasant and many are not directly associated with flowers. Foliage, fruit and bark can be fragrant and often need to be bruised or rubbed to bring out the perfume. Heavy rain showers in warm weather can induce the richest odours, mingled with damp earthy smells. As evening falls, the heady perfumes are released to tantalize and charm as they drift across the darkening air.

Experiencing scent is a very personal sensation. No two people will necessarily find the same fragrance attractive. The strong odour of privet *(Ligustrum)* is profoundly distasteful to me yet others find its dense cloying smell both rich and sweet. Take care when mixing scents. Use scented plants sparingly so as not to confuse these important sensations. One perfume may not mix with another and an overall, blended fragrance from the garden loses the individual charm associated with a single source.

*Right The elegantly structured flowers of Lonicera periclymenum emit a most beautiful scent, at its strongest in the late evening. The delicate shades of pink and cream flowers are followed by rich red berries. Grow it around a doorway or entrance so that visitors experience the all-pervading perfume. (The climber may also be used as a ground-cover.)*

*Left Rosa "Adelaide d'Orléans" decorates this doorway with clusters of pink-cream flowers. For many people roses are the ultimate in scented flowers although not all have strong perfumes. Some of the more recent introductions dispel the idea that perfume is lacking in modern roses: R. "Fritz Nobis", R. "Wendy Cussons" and R. "Prima Ballerina" are all strongly scented.*

*Above The sail-like leaves of Musa float above a haze of tobacco plants (Nicotiana). The flowers are borne profusely over summer, releasing their sweet fragrance as the sun sinks. N. alata has the strongest perfume and comes in numerous varieties, bred primarily for colour rather than scent.*

### FLOWERS AND FOLIAGE FOR SCENT

For scented flowers early in the season use *Viburnum × burkwoodii*, *Tulipa sylvestris*, *Hyacinthus orientalis*, *Muscari armeniacum*, *Corylopsis sinensis* or *Osmanthus delavayi*.
For summer scents use *Nicotiana alata* (and various *Nicotiana* sp.), *Lathyrus odoratus*, *Phlox maculata*, *Lilium regale*, *Wisteria sinensis* and *Lavandula spica*.
For autumn scents try *Cyclamen europaeum*, *Lilium henryi*, *Lonicera halliana* or *Verbena rigida*, or use *Hamamelis mollis*, *Mahonia japonica*, *Lonicera fragrantissima* and *Sarcococca humilis*.
For aromatic foliage use *Rosmarinus officinalis*, *Helichrysum angustifolium*, *Mentha spicata*, *Choisya ternata* or *Gaultheria procumbens*.

**Left** *The romantic notion of the overgrown garden complete with sweet-smelling roses and flowering arbours is achievable in most gardens but is most effective on a grand scale. The damp scents of uncharted shade, undergrowth and dew-covered flowers are evocative, rich and tantalizing.*

# COTTAGE GARDENS

The popular view of cottage gardens tends to ignore the reality – that they were primarily functional gardens. The image of soft-focus borders filled with romantic flowers is only part of the story. These are recent recreations of an ideal, stemming from increased leisure time, improved living standards and freely available produce in the supermarket. The original cottage gardens were fairly limited in size and combined an element of self-sufficiency with decorative flowers (largely escapees from surrounding fields and hedgerows). Every available inch would have been used – hence this contemporary translation of a profusion of colour, shape and texture.

The cottage garden has now become the antithesis of formality. Materials are simple, or cobbled together from available leftovers on site – any stones, pebbles, bricks or timber found locally. The shrubs and flowers tumble across pathways, clamber around doorways and generally colonize the garden in unruly masses. Clouds of delicate roses, drooping racemes of *Wisteria*, blue spikes of *Delphinium* and scented frills of *Dianthus* contribute to the dream-like image of a cottage garden. But a true cottage garden takes the functional fruit and vegetables and mixes them with the flowers. For the flowers, go back to the species plants and old cultivars, instead of seeking new varieties. In this way, you can sample the delights of the true cottage garden.

*Right* Roses around the cottage door have featured on too many chocolate boxes, and have become a cliché in gardening terms. But climbing roses studded with colourful flowers are difficult to beat. Use scented and vigorous species for heightened effect or combine them with other climbing plants such as honeysuckle (Lonicera) or clematis, to disguise their bare thorny stems.

*Left* This flower border epitomizes the look of the cottage garden with its strong colours in seemingly ad hoc arrangements. The combination of textures and colours is in a sense naive, improvised and yet effusive.

## PLANTS FOR INFORMAL PLANTINGS

Use plant material that will either ramble, or has an open, random branching network to create an informal, spontaneous appearance. Shrubs such as *Buddleia davidii*, *Kerria japonica*, *Philadelphus* "Beauclerk" or *Syringa vulgaris*. Plant around these species with *Alchemilla mollis*, *Aster novi-belgii*, *Lilium regale*, *Dianthus* (many forms) and *Campanula carpatica*. For height use *Delphinium* (various forms), *Digitalis purpurea* or *Althaea rosea*. Roses are particularly useful and appropriate. Choose from *Rosa moyesii* "Geranium", *R.* "Boule de Neige", or *R. gallica officinalis*. For climbers or ramblers try *R.* "Albéric Barbier", *R.* "Albertine" or *R.* "Dorothy Perkins", with wisterias or clematis alongside. Sprinkle *Aquilegia vulgaris*, *Alyssum saxatile*, *Geranium pratense*, *Hemerocallis* (various forms), *Paeonia lactiflora* and *Lupinus* (various forms) amongst the other border plants, filling the gaps and increasing the flowering potential.

**Left** *The thistle-like flowering heads of* Centaurea pulchra *"Major" dominate this subdued border, which relies on purples and green-blues for its effect. The incorporation of happy accidents within the border plays a part. Allow things like self-seeding to happen – part of the enjoyment of gardening in this style stems from allowing things to happen and then deciding whether they are appropriate or acceptable.*

# THE ROSE GARDEN

Species roses are the ancestors of modern roses. The flowers are simple with five petals although some double forms exist. They are strongly scented and bear numerous flowers in summer followed later by large hips. Old roses arise from species roses, usually as hybrids. They form deciduous shrubs with their scent as a major characteristic. Their flowers are complex, multi-petalled and sometimes quartered.

Hybrid teas have a much longer flowering season than the majority of roses. Their main use is for cut flowers and the shape and form of these plants takes a secondary role. Floribunda roses have a dense branching pattern and their flowers are borne in large clusters. Their scent is not usually strong; they are used mainly as decorative flowering plants for the border.

Modern shrub roses are hybrids produced from species and old roses. They are appropriate for specimen planting, often reaching 2m (6ft or so) high and spreading in arching, flowering garlands. They are occasionally scented but their chief virtue is that they produce flowers throughout the summer. Some may be used for hedging or to give structure to larger borders. Climbers and ramblers carry fragrant flowers, often quite large. They may be used for training over free-standing walls and pergolas, over old tree stumps, or against the house if supported. Miniature and standard forms of roses are also commonly used for specific effects.

*Below* Roses can be used to ramble through trees. Often this technique is adopted with over-mature specimen trees or with species of little particular merit. The clusters of bright flowers of Rosa "Madame Isaac Pereire" clamber through high branches.

*Left* Rosa glauca *is a species rose with delicate pink and white simple flowers. It is a favourite in colour-themed gardens as its purple-grey foliage and purple stems are a major feature, lasting much longer than the relatively short-lived flowers.*

*Right* This combination of roses with delphiniums is probably the most successful method of using the plants. Rose gardens with pure stands of roses can look stark and sober even when in full flower. They simply become a display area to show off blooms rather than a sensual and exciting garden of scent, colour and texture. The combination of lemon, white, blue and pink is not one which would normally spring to mind but with a pastel range many more colour combinations are possible.

## CHOOSING ROSES

The wide variety of roses now available makes choice very difficult. By deciding on a particular, desired characteristic the field can be narrowed. For scent, therefore, choose from *Rosa* "Golden Showers" (climber), *R.* "Frühlingsgold" (modern shrub), *R.* "Madame Pierre Oger" (Bourbon), *R.* "Elizabeth of Glamis" (floribunda) and *R. rugosa* "Frau Dagmar Hartopp" (species).

For rose hips choose from *R. moyesii* "Geranium" (species), *R. gallica* "Officinalis" (species) and *R. damascena*.

For simple flowers choose freely from the species roses or more specifically *R.* "Complicata" (Gallica), *R.* "Ballerina" (hybrid musk) and *R.* "Escapade" (floribunda).

For cut flowers the most appropriate are the hybrid tea roses with long stems and individual flowers. Choose from *R.* "Pascali", *R.* "Blue Moon", *R.* "Elizabeth Harkness", *R.* "Superstar" or *R.* "Peace". Also try *R.* "The Fairy" (floribunda) and *R.* "Will Scarlet".

Foliage effect is more pronounced within the species roses. Use *R. glauca* (formerly *R. rubrifolia)* for purple-silver leaf and stem, *R. spinosissima* for fern-like leaves and extremely bristly stems. The bright foliage of *R. rugosa* is also most attractive.

Climbing and rambling roses are essentially the same. They are useful for growing up through trees or over buildings. Both need supporting and tying. Again the choice is great but *R.* "Maigold", *R.* "New Dawn", *R.* "Albertine", the thornless *R.* "Zephirine Drouhin", *R.* "Kiftsgate", *R.* "Dorothy Perkins" and *R.* "Rambling Rector" all make fine plants. At the other extreme are the miniatures, suitable for raised beds and containers. Go and see them in flower at your local nursery and choose from among the many varieties which could include *R.* "Josephine", *R.* "Little Flirt", *R.* "Dwarfking", *R.* "Memory Lane", *R.* "Little Sir Echo", *R.* "Littlest Angel" and *R.* "Green Ice".

# BORDER PLANTING

The garden border is often seen as an area of ground allotted to growing collected plants. A wide variety of species may be included with little unity between them. Occasionally in the wide-ranging style referred to as "cottage garden" these vague plant associations work by chance or accident.

In planning a border these elements must be identified. An underlying structure must be arranged initially. Shrubs, hedging or larger-scale plants may be planted to provide this. Garden walls or fences may be used in a similar way, perhaps draped with climbing plants. Against these anchors, plants or structures, various plant associations may be arranged. Structural planting may be neutral to allow more colourful or dramatic foliage to be displayed to greater effect. Alternatively structural planting may introduce a colour, texture or shape which may inspire a plant association.

Rather than adopting the traditional style, which demands low planting at the front of the border and high planting at the rear, use sculpted groups of planting, including different shapes or patterns, standing in low ground-cover. The space around the plants can then be explored, depth is introduced with shadows and filtering light. Alternatively choose a theme of foliage or flower colour or shape. Try borders of plants with sword-shaped leaves such as iris *(Iris sibirica)*, red hot poker *(Kniphofia)*, *Crocosmia* and cabbage palm *(Cordyline australis)*.

**Above** The delicate structured flowers of Aquilegia *decorate the edge of the path with colour and intricate pattern. The flowers are contrasted against the richer green of climbing hydrangea (Hydrangea petiolaris), which has a much stronger texture and introduces deep shade within its flowering branches.*

**Left** *The border is framed by the creeper-covered house to the rear and the well-tended lawn to the front, from where the border must be viewed for greatest impact.*

**Far left** *This formal quadrangle is endowed with a dream-like quality by the strong pinks of* Dahlia *planted to the exclusion of all else. The dark greens of the foliage beyond make the colour much stronger.*

# COLOUR-THEMED PLANTING

Colour can be manipulated to create atmosphere in the garden, particularly in summer when flowers are abundant and alight with colour. Single-colour borders are particularly effective but benefit from an injection of colour from another part of the spectrum, otherwise their hues can become monotonous and flat. Use blues and purple shades for coolness, reds, oranges, crimsons or yellows for warmth or brightness, and whites for elegance and mystic charm. Colours such as pinks, lemon-yellows and pastel shades can be planted alongside ice-cream-coloured combinations that are both subtle and fresh-looking.

Use foliage colour for contrast or to heighten an effect. Dark yew *(Taxus baccata)* behind white flowers produces a mysterious, almost funereal quality to the planting. Silvery-grey foliage with white looks frosted and magical. Yellow-green or variegated leaves key in the foliage to the searing yellow of shining flowers. Mix colours together for dynamic effect. Reds, oranges, burgundies and warm yellows suggest burning heat; aim for rippling fire colours blowing in the breeze alongside spiked or spear-headed foliage like flames. Mix blues from palest ice to midnight shades, lose royal purples against dark foliage or allow strong lilacs and emeralds to vibrate with colour. Be prepared to experiment with colour and do not expect instant success first time round. Colour themes can take years to perfect, and flowering times cannot always be guaranteed to work by the book or as envisaged.

*Right The colour scheme for a border need not rely on flower alone. Foliage is rich in colour that can contrast or complement flowers. Shades of leaf colour vary from black-green to yellow-white with rich blue-greens and silver-greens too. Flower colour can be used for highlighting colour variations or nuances in foliage to create a mood that pervades the border or the complete garden.*

**Below** *The value of a dark background against which vibrant colours can be dramatically displayed is exemplified here. The black-green of yew (*Taxus baccata*) is an ideal foil for the searing yellows of* Verbascum, Solidago *and* Coreopsis. *The silvery spikes of* Verbascum *are framed in high contrast and the tiny sulphurous flowers are picked out as individual flashes of colour.*

**Right** *The vivid oranges and reds revel in the bright sunshine and the delicate structure of* Lilium *flowers dance above the general mass as if caught in currents of rising air. The use of yellow flowers in the distance cools the view and the border seems somehow longer, almost lost in a light summer haze.*

# OVERHEAD FLOWERS

Climbing plants play an important role in any garden, as their flowers are often large, dramatic and exotic. They can be grown against the walls of a house but if you create supports for them within the garden, you then see them at their best. Pergolas or archways provide light frames that enable the plants to clamber or ramble high into the air, their flowers cascading down above our heads. The structures can be decorative in themselves and commonly consist of timber, usually stained, or of a timber frame with brick or stone supports. The great beauty of these structures lies in their mature planted appearance when only a hint of the framework is evident beneath trusses of flower or foliage. With heavy pruning, the climbing plants can be thinned and forced against the structure, expressing its major decorative features, whether patterned trellis, intricate jointing or whimsical finials. Much lighter frames of tubular steel may be quickly lost against the stems of climbers, allowing the plant material to float in mid-air. Or chains can be draped between uprights to allow climbers to droop in flowery swags.

**Far left** *These solid timber beams rest on brick supports above decorative flower borders. Their weathered greys and fine grain are most attractive without the benefit of planting. Indeed, few are planted with climbers as the heavy shade they cast would restrict the planting possibilities beneath.*

**Left** *This spectacular arch of wisteria (Wisteria sinensis "Alba") allows the best qualities of the climber to be displayed. The twisted branches and stems – a principal feature of this plant – are surpassed only by the graceful racemes of honey-scented flowers. The supports are hardly noticeable.*

**Above** *An unusual use of Cercis siliquastrum, the Judas Tree. The tree has been allowed to grow to a height of 2.5m (8ft) before being trained along a framework tied back to the retaining wall. The rose-pink flowers in late spring are an attractive alternative to the more common flowering cherries, although not as profusely carried. They are also easily damaged by late frosts in colder areas.*

# THE FORMAL GARDEN

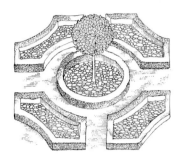

Formality in the garden can be interpreted in many ways. Formal gardens can take many different forms: grand avenues, parterres, knot gardens, vistas and geometric pools come instantly to mind.

Many of the great gardens of the world are formal, amongst them those of the Alhambra, Versailles and Hampton Court. In terms of style, the gardens at Hidcote Manor or at Sissinghurst can still be described as formal, yet their character is quite different. What all these gardens have in common is scale. They occupy large areas or depend on long vistas for effect.

### SHAPE AND PATTERN

Formality in garden or landscape design is symbolic of man's domination over nature and his environment. It communicates order and organization impressing man's achievement upon us.

The French and Italian influence on garden design brought formal layout to a high art form of geometric balance in Western classicism. The main elements were enclosed, directional avenues, large open spaces, parterres, water in cascades, canals or ornamental pools and, where possible, grand staircases. The European gardens of Versailles, Karlsruhe and Potsdam embody this style and are truly grand in scale and imagination.

Symmetry is important to these layouts, introducing balance and harmony. These formidable plans usually emanated from, or revolved around, a residence, usually a formal palace, château or castle. The formal lines of the garden related to the built form and the façades, creating a plinth or setting for the property and translating its vertical form into horizontal decoration.

Intricate parterres occupied the terraces in the vicinity of great houses, and were intended to be viewed from first- or second-floor level, where the great entertaining suites were located. The eye would be directed far into the distance from this same viewpoint, along hedge or tree-lined avenues towards some obelisk, folly or focal point beyond. An underlying geometry controlled the planting, restrained by careful pruning, raised edges or low hedging and colourful bedding or gravels decorated the patterns of the parterre.

Away from the terrace planting should be restricted to foliage plants, shrubs and trees. Little colour is evident traditionally and the herbaceous

*This dramatic entrance to formal gardens manages to restrict the view and emphasize the spectacular planting beyond. As the vista opens out you are able to look around and appreciate the complete effect. For passers-by, a keyhole glimpse through the solid stone wall is tantalizing and irresistible, inviting exploration.*

borders of the English style are something of a compromise.

The dynamic forms and colour schemes of herbaceous planting do not fit in with true formality and symmetry although the material may well be arranged within a formal bed, against clipped hedges or even balanced with other borders. Their beauty lies in dramatic foliage and romantic combinations of flower and colour.

Near the house the treatment was mainly hard becoming softer, though still controlled and moulded into the far distance. These elements still exist in contemporary garden design. The main feature in the majority of gardens is the house, with formal geometric shapes and façades. Somehow those patterns and forms must be reconciled to the garden surrounding the property, which is essentially soft and organic in character.

The terrace or entertaining area of the garden is still one of the main

**Above** *The formal lawn is characteristic of English style. Trimmed to perfection close to the house, the lawn often slips into wild verges or woodland at some distance, or a ha-ha allows a continuous view into parkland beyond.*

**Right** *The exotic splendour of the Alhambra uses water as a major influence. Reflective pools or elegant fountains have a cooling effect using light, sound or moving pattern alongside dark foliage.*

**Far right** *This small courtyard-style garden is carefully planted with a range of muted evergreens, permitting the paving patterns and the contrived effect of* trompe l'oeil *to dominate the design. The rich honey colour of the stone contrasts well with terracotta, and is repeated in the containers and brickwork. The gravel dressing and the dark green bench complete a harmonious combination.*

features of the modern garden and here formal elements can be freely introduced. Paving patterns take scale, proportion and geometry from the property creating a transition zone between house and garden where hard surfaces meet and inter-relate with soft plant material. Symmetrical arrangements are well suited to this section of the garden creating strong axes from window views along the terrace and out into the garden beyond. Pots, ornaments or statuary may channel the eye into the chosen vista, which might end with specimen planting, water or sculpture.

## FORMAL PLANTING

Planting should be retained in geometric beds, usually in a formal style. perhaps using roses or lavender, with clipped box hedging. The creation of vistas works by continuing views along pre-determined routes. Clipped hedging such as yew *(Taxus baccata)*, beech *(Fagus sylvatica)*, hornbeam *(Carpinus betulus)* or holly *(Ilex aquifolium)* identifies space with architectural precision. Tapestry hedges mixing various species are useful for introducing colour and texture, contrasting the copper leaves of beech against the velvet green of yew.

Figurative or geometric topiary is only one step away. Exciting forms and shapes can be incorporated into hedging, and topiary is seen at its best when the dark leafy forms are contrasted with terrace paving or with the smooth green sward of a formal lawn.

The lawn beneath or around the formal elements should be mown to a smooth texture, restricted to bold rectangular shapes and used as a foil for the architecture, ornament and formal planting.

Trees with strong form or shape should be used in avenue planting. Lime *(Tilia × europea)*, horse chestnut *(Aesculus hippocastanum)*, beech *(Fagus sylvatica)*, or plane *(Platanus × hybrida)* are frequently used although maple *(Acer platanoides)*, sweet chestnut *(Castanea sativa)* and oak *(Quercus robur)* are also common. For small scale vistas frame with Irish yew *(Taxus baccata* "Fastigiata")*, cherry *(Prunus avium* or *P. subhirtella)*, holly *(Ilex aquifolium)* or rowan *(Sorbus aucuparia)*.

Take care when choosing ornament or statuary; there are many inadequate artefacts now available. Sundials, bird baths, vases and cherubs are mass-produced in poor imitations of stone. These elements ae often too small in scale to act as a focus of attention. Even in restricted space aim for bold and dramatic elements, choose terracotta or stone pots of some magnitude, overflowing with exuberant plant material, or use specimen plants or a water feature. Experiment with asymmetry contrasted with symmetry. Contemporary sculpture is often set off well in a formal landscape. It proclaims its presence and strength against a rigid framework. Sculpture is complemented by mobile reflections in the rippling mirrored surface of water.

Pots containing clipped bay *(Laurus nobilis)* or box *(Buxus semper-virens)* may be arranged formally in quite tiny spaces and *trompe l'oeil* can create classical vistas on bare walls. Furniture should be rigid and strong, such as timber benches in weathered hardwood or painted softwoods. White or elegant aquamarine are the favourite colour options. Fixed seating works well here to take advantage of particular views or focal points.

Generally the formal garden is regarded as a maintenance liability. Hedges must be pristinely trimmed, decorative bedding effects are changed seasonally, lawns need regular mowing and frequently planted rose beds need a great deal of pruning. These gardens certainly need man's intervention if they are to succeed. Much of the work though is associated with scale; once the scale is reduced, their work requirement is not necessarily greater than any other garden style.

## HET LOO, APELDOORN, HOLLAND

The formal gardens of Het Loo capture all the important elements of this type of garden. Long avenues and vistas are controlled by rigid planting; water is retained in severe geometric shapes and wide gravel walks are lined with formal beds. Statuary, planting or decorative fountains close long views with a dramatic flourish and planting is restrained and restricted by heavy pruning. The scale on which these theatrical effects are produced is vast, yet with careful planning it is possible to reproduce formality on a more domestic, smaller scale.

Symmetrical balance is important and illusion or the trickery of *trompe l'oeil* is a valuable asset. But even in the smallest garden, try not to scale statuary or ornament down too much otherwise its whole effect will be lost. Formal lawns, clipped hedging and topiary are all high-maintenance elements. Use the texture of gravels or the geometric lines of trellis for climbing plants as possible alternatives. Formal arrangements of containers and decorative pots can also be used if space is very restricted.

**Left** *This narrow canal feature decorates the wide gravel walk with the directional emphasis towards the ornate fountain curtailing the view. Surfaces are restricted to flat colour with little texture: the ornament is contained within the main stone feature and decorative trellis while flowering plants are arranged behind neatly clipped box hedges.*

**Above** *The massive trunks of beech (Fagus sylvatica) dominate this walk with its cathedral-like proportions. Green shadowy light percolates down to a russet, leaf-littered floor and the eye is drawn to the specimen tree at the end of the avenue, bathed in bright sunlight.*

## SCHEME FOR A FORMAL GARDEN

1 *Cordyline australis*
2 *Buxus sempervirens*
3 *Fagus sylvatica*
4 *Juniperus communis* "Hibernica"
5 *Laurus nobilis*

**Above** *This formal courtyard or parterre centres on a simple octagonal water feature with a rather diminutive gilded cherub as the centrepiece. The main interest comes from the planting treatment, clipped and trained in a rigid architectural style. The simplicity of the gravel and the dark, subdued foliage are necessary to this decorative treatment.*

# ORNAMENTS AND BUILDINGS

Ornamentation and decorative architecture are essential adjuncts to the formal garden. They give meaning to vistas, avenues and walks and decorate fountains, balustrades and terraces. Ornament should be bold and symmetrical as this style relies on the creation of highly structured spaces that must be decorated with strength and purpose. Stone vases, urns, baroque statues and classical figures are appropriate. Spouting cupids, sundials and finials must fit in with the grand scale. All too often contemporary reproductions do not attempt to match the scale or detail evident in original works. If you use statues, position them boldly standing as if in judgement or as sentinels either side of an arch or gateway. Further from the house where informality takes over, use the same features incorporated into planting or in shade – a subterranean grotto, if you have the space, or an underground lair for sprites or shadowy gods. Decorate them with pebbles, rich patterns or materials like some underground jewel.

Gazebos and summerhouses may be ornamented in the classical manner as pure follies, empty but highly decorative. Some may be visible for miles around, important pointers or markers in the landscape, peeping through the woodland canopy or crowning hilltops with viewing platforms.

**Left** *This summerhouse has a magnificent classical façade, albeit unnecessary for its function. The lichen-covered tawny stone contrasts well with the cool white interior and the reflected image peeps back from the dark water beneath the water lilies. The bankside planting of Iris creates a frame around the formal pool while the dark trees beyond provide height and structure.*

**Above** *The cold stone features of this rose-draped figure are warmed by filtered sunshine. The lichen, moss and weathered stone add interest and character, giving a sense of belonging. These effects come only with time, as stone attracts this kind of patina with age – concrete replicas do not mellow so easily.*

### IDEAS FOR POSITIONING

When using formal ornamentation, adopt dramatic or theatrical imagery. Either scale itself, or the emphasis on scale, is important. Create vistas framed by classical figures, as sentinels guarding restricted entrances or gates. Use statues against the smooth green of trimmed hedges, create arenas or open-air theatres and amphitheatres. Ornament may be used structurally as architectural decoration providing spaces or rooms which need no roof.
Create rhythm or a sense of perspective by the accurate placing of artefacts, equidistant from each other, along some important avenue or walk. Use vases, urns or finials to give extra height and power to walls, balustrades and plinths.
Stone is an expensive material but usually the best in its various colours and textures. It grows richer and more interesting as time passes. Concrete can be washed or painted with live yoghurt or liquid manure to attract lichen and thereby combat its sterility.

**Left** *The dark wrestling figures emerge from the still pool as if to herald some great arrival. The quiet surface reflects a kind of melancholy from the towering trees of the formal avenue. The colours are melancholic: greens, browns and shadowy tones – almost black giving a strong sense of atmosphere. However, the plinth which holds the statue is highly visible. Had the water level been raised, the concrete or stone painted black, it would have receded more easily or been lost in the murky shade.*

# THE SECRET GARDEN

In creating formal spaces, which are often rigid and on a grand scale, there is a strong need for a contrast in atmosphere, scale and function. The concept of a secret garden allows retreats, hideaways or simply quiet areas to be tucked into the grand design. These places rely on their concealment for their charm and not being immediately obvious, visitors may never be aware of their existence unless introduced to them. For the initiated these secret gardens become all the more valuable – there is a sense of adventure or discovery in happening across some subterranean grotto, leafy glade or shadowy dell. This, combined with an atmosphere of privacy or enclosure, rewards the visitor with the pleasurable feeling that this secret garden was intended only for him or her. In comparison with more formal layouts, the need for enclosure and privacy demands a reduction in scale, symmetry and regularity. There should be a tangible experience of passing over a threshold – almost a feeling of invasion as if trespassing on private property, so the world outside can be closed off as escapism takes over. Often a walled garden works successfully with restricted entry and, therefore, restricted views. Gateways or doors can be left tantalizingly ajar, primed for further investigation. Hedges or dense planted screens offer this same privacy, allowing light and sound to filter through with a whispered message from the other side. To make a contrast, introduce a profusion of colour as relief to the stark formality elsewhere or include a bench or seat to invite relaxation and contemplation.

*Left* The sunlit gravel path leads to a distant statue through a series of planted spaces. Restricted visual information is given through the narrow archways which hint at riches beyond. They invite investigation and reward with colourful planting. These avenues or walkways to hidden spaces are almost impossible to ignore. Whilst formality underlies this layout, the edges of the pathway are soft and indefinite. The planting is tall and dreamy, and climbing foliage drapes the wall. Severity and contrivance are set aside and Nature is allowed some influence.

**Left** *The doorway frames the view beautifully into rose-filled gardens. Clipped box* (Buxus sempervirens) *and climbing hydrangea* (Hydrangea petiolaris) *give foreground interest and texture, to make the vista shine through with light and colour. At the far end of these richly planted borders, a bench looks back to the point of entry. The temptation to close the door and lock out the rest of the world is overpowering.*

**Above** *This impression of a decorated courtyard beyond the stone wall is intriguing and inviting. The scale is domestic and welcoming. Rich textured plants decorate the pathways and trees offer cool shade. The enclosing walls offer privacy and protection as if part of some large house or monastery.*

# TOPIARY

Topiary – the art of trimming trees and shrubs into ornamental or architectural shapes – can, in its most basic form, be applied to basic hedge pruning. But it can also develop into fabulous animals, geometric forms and intricate green structures. Many early examples of knot gardens or parterres used fine clipped hedging such as box *(Buxus sempervirens)* to identify shapes and patterns in low relief. On a much grander scale, yew *(Taxus baccata)* may be used. Both of these species respond well to hard pruning, producing fine, dense textures as a result. By restricting or forcing these plants into chosen shapes, the material may be used as a sculptural element, creating enclosure, framing views, decorating with exotic finials, fantastic beasts or obelisks. Hedges form walls to enclose a garden room and topiary furnishes these with interesting decoration. This form of expression is best suited to the grand scale of garden design, where the rich emerald of formal lawns supports the dark olive of clipped hedging. On the smaller scale, complex shapes, figures or patterns are difficult to read or view. Privet *(Ligustrum ovalifolium)* is often used as hedging and patiently nurtured into decorative shapes. The open texture of this species, dictated by its larger leaf, means that the infrastructure or supporting branches are clearly visible. The denser growth of yew and box, on the other hand, ensures that visually the foliage itself expresses the shape. Almost any shape or form can be replicated but the strongest are the primary forms of pure geometry.

*Left* The solid forms of topiary effectively enclose the garden space and channel the view through a narrow arch to give a glimpse of colour and excitement beyond. The foliage texture expresses the shapes in subtle tones of light and shade against the neutral backdrop of the main hedge, and the size of these elements works well given the overall scale of the garden.

*Above* These unusual pot shapes frame the view back to the elegant house. The dense texture works well against the hard stone paving and still manages to create a softening effect.

*Right* The contrast of leaf textures works in a similar way to topiary. In this case the rigid shapes are retaining walls covered in ivy (Hedera colchica) *and* creeping fig (Ficus pumila). *The terracotta pots introduce a touch of brightness and the plants in them can be changed seasonally to alter the colour scheme.*

# KNOTS AND PARTERRES

The grand formal layouts of parterres or the smaller intricate knot gardens both rely on similar materials for effect. The hard materials are most frequently gravels, often of various colours or types or, with the knot gardens in particular, brick or small stone units. Box *(Buxus sempervirens)* is the most common hedging plant although scented species such as lavender *(Lavandula)* are also popular. Designed to be viewed from above, formal parterres dominate the terraces around many of the great European palaces and châteaux. They expressed grandeur whilst the knot gardens of England depicted a more domestic scene of herbs, aromatic plants and flowers. The patterns and shapes in knot gardens were widely copied in the sixteenth century when this particular style was at its peak. The more intricate the knot pattern, the less chance there would be to include infill planting. More open designs were often adapted for use with the preferred flowers or herbs of the time.

Contemporary knots or parterres should work best when borrowed from the original styles and patterns but not slavishly copied. Experiment with abstract shapes or simplified geometry and with fresh colour schemes or interesting foliage textures. A wide variety of gravels or crushed rocks is also currently available. Alternatively, consider the qualities of pebbles, cobbles, decorative mulches and intricate brick or tile paving.

*Left* *The planting in this Italian parterre hugs the ground, radiating from a central pool. The main punctuation is provided by the terracotta pots, strategically placed at important junctions in the pattern. They also help to frame the view out from the terrace to the valley beyond.*

*Right* *This elegant knot garden shows the distinct contrast in scale with the much grander parterre. The detail of the knot is picked out in foliage greens, while topiary spheres add interest and shape. The coloured gravel echoes the stone of the house, and the terrace and elevation work well as a unified concept. I would be tempted to remove the sundial which tends to confuse the attractive simplicity of the terrace.*

*Bottom right* *The perfectly trimmed hedging, subtle planting and the effects of light and shade add a magical, almost surreal quality to this majestic parterre. The neutral shade and texture of the gravel paving allows the richness of the hedging to dominate the terrace. Elegant obelisks decorate the simple lines and the controlled colour of the infill planting provides delicate filigree stippling when viewed from above. The planting is arranged symmetrically around the central axis but each section of the design is different. White timber containers continue the formal lines out across the gravel. Often, in warmer regions, the containers arranged across the terraces would contain citrus fruits, their dark foliage contrasting with the luminous white paint.*

### CHOOSING HEDGING MATERIAL

In creating these decorative gardens a major influence on their design and final appearance is the choice of hedging material. Box *(Buxus sempervirens)* is probably the most popular choice as it can easily be trimmed and shaped on the small scale. Other species such as lavender *(Lavandula spica)*, santolina *(Santolina chamaecyparissus)* or germander *(Teucrium chamaedrys)* will provide scent and a colour contrast. Within the shapes created, a wide variety of species may be used either decoratively or functionally, or both. Planting in general tends to be low to avoid confusing the overall shape or pattern. At important junctions or corners a specimen plant may be used – either clipped box or perhaps a rose or bay *(Laurus nobilis)*. Use herbs such as rosemary *(Rosmarinus officinalis)*, sage *(Salvia officinalis)*, hyssop *(Hyssopus officinalis)* and lavender between. Tall species such as fennel *(Foeniculum vulgare)*, angelica *(Angelica archangelica)* or tree onion *(Allium cepa)* should be used with care, either massed together or in restricted areas. Use lady's mantle *(Alchemilla mollis)*, chamomile *(Anthemis nobilis)* or violet *(Viola odorata)* as ground-covering plants. For flowers use roses such as *Rosa gallica officinalis*, *R. damascena* or *R. rubiginosa* or alternatively perennials like primula *(Primula, various)*, pinks *(Dianthus)*. foxglove *(Digitalis)* or paeony *(Paeonia)*

# THE PLANT DIRECTORY

*In the following plant guide I have attempted to pick out a short list of some of the best plants for each style of garden in this book. By best I mean interesting foliage, attractive habit and exciting flower colour or scent. There are of course many thousands of plants to choose from, and your final choice must depend on the aspect of your garden, its soil and climate.*

## Key

FOL = Foliage garden
WA = Water garden
ALL = All-seasons garden
C = City garden
W = Wild garden
ALF = Al fresco garden
E = Edible garden
O = Oriental garden
FLR = Flower garden
FOR = Formal garden

*Aesculus hippocastanum*
**Common horse chestnut**
TREE (DECIDUOUS) (GREECE AND ALBANIA)
The common horse chestnut is often taken for granted. Next time you pass a specimen in flower, take a close look at the flower spikes. They are almost as exotic as orchids. Surely this is one of the most beautiful large trees hardy in temperate regions. The stout "candles" of white flowers appear in late spring. The chestnut makes a magnificent large avenue tree or parkland specimen. (Up to 30m – 100ft.) FLR, C.

*Buxus sempervirens*
**Common box**
SHRUB OR TREE (EVERGREEN) (S. EUROPE, N. AFRICA AND W. ASIA)
The beloved box has a multitude of uses. The masses of small dark green leaves are an excellent foil for more extravagant foliage. It responds well to hard clipping and is, with yew, the standard plant for topiary. It also makes an excellent low formal hedge. (Left to grow, it will reach 10m – 33ft). For really dwarf hedges, choose the slow-growing form "Suffruticosa", also known as edging box. FOL, O, C.

*Carpinus betulus*
**Common hornbeam**
TREE (DECIDUOUS) (EUROPE AND ASIA MINOR)
This beautiful and versatile tree is easy to grow. Plant as single specimens (when it will normally grow to well over 25m – 80ft) as an avenue tree or use for hedging including pleaching (rather like a hedge on stilts). The silver fluted trunk of a mature hornbeam is most distinctive; the foliage in many ways resembles that of beech. Two upright-growing cultivars ("Columnaris" and "Fastigiata") make excellent formal avenue trees, smaller in stature than the parent species. W.

*Fagus sylvatica*
**Common beech**
TREE (DECIDUOUS) (EUROPE)
A noble tree indeed. As a parkland specimen, where it will reach 30m (100ft), it is unrivalled, especially on alkaline soils. The rich golden-copper of its autumn foliage is hard to beat. As long as the soil is well drained, it will tolerate extremes of both alkalinity and acidity. Beech makes a magnificent avenue tree, creating a cool, atmospheric tunnel of dense foliage. A beech hedge will also delight. When clipped, beech retains its golden-brown dead leaves throughout winter, only shed when the new leaves push them off in spring. There are many named forms including "Riversii" (a good large-leaved copper beech), *F.s. heterophylla* (a delightful cut-leaved form) and "Dawyck" (a tall columnar variety). FOL, W.

*Ilex aquifolium*
**Common holly**
TREE OR SHRUB (EVERGREEN) (EUROPE, N. AFRICA TO CHINA)
Left alone the holly will reach over 20m (66ft). Innumerable cultivars are available with variously shaped and coloured leaves. Female clones, of course, provide the added bonus of red (occasionally yellow) berries in winter. Holly can be clipped (as they are in the tight, tall domes in the Rose Garden at The Royal Botanic Garden at Kew) or left to make a dark evergreen backcloth or screen. ALL, FOL, W, C.

*Laurus nobilis*
**Bay laurel**
SHRUB OR TREE (EVERGREEN) (MEDITERRANEAN)
This is the laurel of the ancients, with aromatic leaves used in cooking. It responds well to being clipped, but may suffer from winter cold in some districts. In milder areas it makes an excellent pot or tub plant and can often be seen clipped into pyramids or standard pom-poms. This use of the bay laurel can give a formal look to even the smallest of gardens. FOL, ALF, E, C.

*Myrtus communis*
**Common myrtle**
SHRUB (EVERGREEN) (S. EUROPE AND W. ASIA)
Myrtle is an aromatic, densely leaved shrub, attaining over 4m (13ft) on a sunny wall. White flowers are borne in mid-to late summer, followed by purple-black berries.

Hard winters may damage or even kill myrtle but in milder areas it is a very useful evergreen. In the formal garden use it as a dark backcloth or medium-sized hedge. Much used in Spanish formal gardens. FLR, FOL, ALF, C.

*Sorbus aucuparia*
**Rowan or mountain ash**
TREE (DECIDUOUS) (EUROPE)
Another familiar tree, but smaller in stature, reaching around 10m (33ft) in height. It has pinnate leaves and large bunches of bright red fruits in autumn that are soon devoured by birds. This is a tough, versatile tree, suitable for small formal avenues, or even for planting along pathways. ALL, W, C.

*Taxus baccata*
**Common yew**
TREE (EVERGREEN-CONIFER) (EUROPE, ALGERIA, MIDDLE EAST)
The small, linear, blackish leaves make this the perfect formal backcloth to ornamental plants, particularly the traditional herbaceous border. Left to grow it will reach 20m (66ft) and live for over 1000 years. The yew has given rise to numerous forms varying in habit and colour.

The form "Fastigiata" (the Irish yew) makes a dense, broad column. "Standishi" is a slow-growing column of golden-yellow leaves – excellent for the small formal garden. FOL, W.

# THE FORMAL GARDEN

*In the formal garden, decorative plants will often take a back seat. Flowering plants may only be used sparingly to provide small explosions of colour interest. Bulbs, roses and bedding plants such as pelargoniums are often used for this purpose. In fact any ornamental plants can be used in this fashion.*

*In the following list I have concentrated on plants that can be used to provide structure and framework in a formal garden and/or can be used for topiary, hedging or avenue planting.*

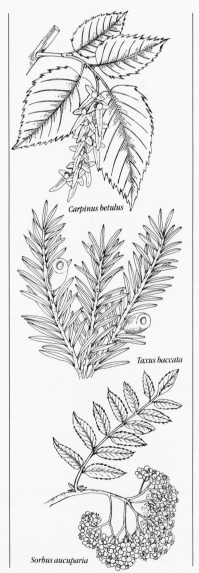

*Carpinus betulus*

*Taxus baccata*

*Sorbus aucuparia*

# THE FOLIAGE GARDEN

*Good foliage plants are most valuable – in any style of garden. I have listed below some of my personal favourites and many with additional decorative attributes that make them very desirable and versatile.*

*Hosta*

*Festuca glauca*

Bergenia cordifolia

*Acanthus spinosus*
**Bear's breeches**
HERBACEOUS PERENNIAL (S. EUROPE)
The handsome, glossy green, divided leaves, up to 90cm (3ft) long, make this one of the most attractive and choice perennials for the foliage garden. (In the Mediterranean you will find it growing as a wasteland and roadside weed.) Given ideal conditions, the invasive roots can be a problem, but in more temperate regions bear's breeches are highly thought of. The prickly flower spikes of soft mauve are perfect above the gold arching foliage. To 1.2m–4ft. ALL, FLR, C.

*Alchemilla mollis*
**Lady's mantle**
HERBACEOUS PERENNIAL (ASIA MINOR)
This plant immediately comes to mind for the foliage garden. The large, pale green hairy leaves are an excellent contrast to grassy or sword-like foliage, and it will grow almost anywhere. To 45cm. O, C.

*Bergenia cordifolia* "Megasea"
PERENNIAL (EVERGREEN) (SIBERIA)
Elephant's ears, as they are often affectionately called, provide a hosta-type effect for those poor gardeners who have to cope with dry soils and strong winds. The creeping rhizomes throw up round leathery leaves as much as 20cm (8in) across. They are often tinged scarlet in autumn and winter. The light mauve-pink flowers appear in spring in dense heads on thick red stems. Bergenias are very tough and good weed-smotherers, growing in sun or shade. To 45cm–18in.

The form "Purpurea" has vivid magenta flowers and large leaves which turn purple in winter. (To 60cm–24in).

Look out for other species and varieties: "Silberlicht" has pure white flowers, "Abendglut" has semi-double

magenta-crimson flowers and rich maroon-tinged foliage in winter. ALL, C.

*Catalpa bignonioides* "Aurea"
**Golden Indian bean tree**
TREE OR SHRUB (DECIDUOUS)
The species makes quite a large, broad-spreading tree with foxglove-like flowers that are white, yellow and purple, followed by long thin bean-like seed pods. The gold-leaved form is slower-growing and smaller in stature. The large, velvety, soft-yellow leaves, however, provide a good textural and colour effect. Not to be grown in exposed areas as the leaves can be torn by the wind. To 4m–13ft. C.

*Cordyline australis*
**Cabbage tree**
SHRUB OR TREE (EVERGREEN) (NEW ZEALAND)
Each branch or stem is crowned by a large dense mass of long slender sword-shaped leaves. (To over 5m–12ft). It is often grown in containers and the overall effect is exotic, palm-like and tropical. ALF, FOR, C.

*Crataegus tanacetifolia*
**Tansy-leaved thorn**
TREE (DECIDUOUS) (ASIA MINOR)
A small (to 5m–17ft) tree with masses of small white flowers in spring followed by yellow fruits. The foliage tops everything off – the leaves are small, quite deeply cut, grey-green and felted. A tough and versatile tree. FLR, O, C.

*Euphorbia characias wulfenii*
**Spurge or milkweed**
PERENNIAL (EVERGREEN) (W. MEDITERRANEAN)
This is a handsome perennial of shrub-like proportions, reaching up to 1.2m (4ft). The erect stems are clothed in narrow blue-green leaves topped in spring with broad spikes of yellowish-green flowers. In mild winters the foliage is retained and is most welcome. ALL, FLR, C.

*Fatsia japonica*
SHRUB (EVERGREEN) (JAPAN)
This evergreen shrub, with very large, polished, dark green palmate leaves, gives an exotic feel to the foliage garden. The milky-white globular flower-heads appear in autumn when little else is in flower. It is often grown as a house plant (wrongly named *Aralia sieboldii*).

This plant is so often planted these days that it is becoming something of a cliché. To 3m–10ft. FLR, ALF, O, C.

*Festuca glauca*
**Blue fescue**
GRASS (EVERGREEN) (EUROPE)
A pretty, densely tufted grass with slender, steel-blue leaves. Use as a ground-cover plant or as an edger, or even as a "spot" plant. Clip over in spring to keep the hummocks tight. To 25cm–10in. FOR, C.

*Gunnera manicata*
HERBACEOUS PERENNIAL (S. BRAZIL)
A gigantic plant, with leaves as much as 1.8m (5ft) across, it is often planted at the waterside or in marshy ground. The flowers are huge bottle-brush spikes of green and brown that appear as the leaves are opening in mid-spring. It is best described as a giant coarse, hairy rhubarb although it is not a member of the rhubarb family. To 2m–6ft or more in leaf. WA.

*Hedera*
**Ivy**
CLIMBER (EVERGREEN)
The genus *Hedera* contains only a small number of species, but the range of foliage forms is so diverse that you could make a stunningly attractive garden with just ivies on their own. It would be virtually maintenance-free and would give all-year-round interest and colour. Ivies will climb or cover the ground. They thrive in any site

or soil. They can be clipped hard or just left to run wild. Try *H. colchica* "Dentata" with large pale green leaves and *H. helix* "Buttercup", a golden-leaved form of the common ivy. ALL, FOR, W, C.

## *Helleborus argutifolius*
PERENNIAL (EVERGREEN) (CORSICA, SARDINIA, BALEARIC ISLANDS)

Surely one of the most beautiful of all foliage plants. The leaves, in three parts, are vaguely prickly, greyish-green and veined. It eventually makes a bushy clump (to 60cm–24in) and the pale green flowers in winter and spring are a wonderful restrained contrast to the subtle foliage. ALL, FLR, C.

## *Hosta*
### Plantain lily
HERBACEOUS PERENNIAL

These are really valuable, low-growing clump-forming perennials, primarily for shade. The oval or rounded leaves come in a wide variety of sizes and colours. Height can vary from a few centimetres to nearly a metre. FLR, O, C, WA.

## *Kniphofia caulescens*
### Red hot poker
PERENNIAL (EVERGREEN) (S. AFRICA)

Most of the red hot pokers are grown for their tall, often bi-coloured, flower spikes. *K. caulescens* is a bit different in that it is mainly grown for its beautiful leaves, that are broad at the base and grass-like at the ends. The new leaves are greyish but turn jade-green during the summer months. Very hardy plants, they grow to 1-2m (3–6ft or so) in flower. The flowers are soft coral initially, turning to green white in early autumn.

## *Mahonia trifoliolata glauca*
SHRUB (EVERGREEN) (SOUTHERN USA & N. MEXICO)

You won't find this plant easily and it won't be cheap to buy when you find it – but as a foliage plant, it is second to none and worth the investment. It needs a warm, sheltered position but given this it will reach up to 2–3m (6–10ft). The leaves are spiny as are all mahonias, but there are

only three leaflets (as the specific epithet suggests) which are conspicuously blue-grey (as the form name indicates). This plant is not very well known but is is a magnificent foliage plant and well worth searching out. ALF.

## *Melianthus major*
SUB-SHRUB (EVERGREEN) (INDIA, S. AFRICA)

One of the most decorative of all foliage plants. The pinnate leaves are grey-green, deeply divided and serrated. The new growth in spring is pale and luminous. The flowers are maroon and tubular, appearing in dense erect spikes in summer. Coming from S. Africa and India, it is not completely hardy in northern temperate regions. However, in a sheltered, sunny, well-drained position it can be surprisingly tolerant of low temperatures. Established plants can grow up to 2m (6ft or more) tall. ALL, ALF.

## *Polystichum setiferum*
### Soft shield fern
HARDY FERN (EUROPE)

Perhaps the most beautiful of all hardy ferns. There are a larger number of named forms with various foliage differences. Especially loved by the Victorians, and then forgotten, ferns are, once again, becoming popular – and rightly so. The soft shield fern will tolerate a certain amount of dryness, and will thrive almost anywhere. The fronds are a soft dull green and the stems are covered in brown shaggy scales. To 1.2m–4ft.

Look out for *P.s.* "Acutilobum" which is especially tough, tolerating even full sun, *P.s.* "Divisilobum" for its elegant deeply divided fronds and the parsley-like *P.s.* "Densum". This fern (and/or one of its many forms) is a must for any foliage garden. W, WA.

## *Rosa glauca*
SPECIES ROSE (CENTRAL AND S. EUROPE)

A rose in a foliage garden may seem strange but *R. glauca* is unique and worth growing just for its foliage. The flowers are single, clear pink and are followed by good red hips, but the foliage is the main attraction. It has a wonderful coppery-

pink hue. Previously known as *R. rubrifolia,* the name still used by some nurserymen. To 2m–6ft. FLR, C.

## *Santolina virens*
### Lavender cotton
SUB-SHRUB (EVERGREEN) (MEDITERRANEAN)

All the lavender cottons are good foliage plants. *S. virens* (or rather *S. rosmarinifolia rosmarinifolia* now) is an attractive dwarf species (to 45cm–18in) with typical thread-like leaves that are intense green in colour. The flower-heads of pale primrose are a genuine and useful bonus – and appear in mid- to late summer. Full sun and well-drained soil is preferred. ALL, FLR, FOR, C.

## *Stachys byzantina*
### Lamb's tongue or lamb's ears
HERBACEOUS PERENNIAL (CAUCASUS TO PERSIA)

A well-known ground-cover plant with its dense mats of woolly grey leaves to no more than 5cm (2in). The small pink flowers are produced on quite a tall stem, wrapped in grey wool. The form "Silver Carpet" is non-flowering and is excellent in association with old roses or as a ground-hugging contrast in the foliage garden. Often listed as *S. lanata* or *S. olympica*. C.

## *Thujopsis dolobrata*
CONIFER (EVERGREEN) (JAPAN)

The sprays of scale-like leaves are shining dark green above and marked with silver-white bands beneath. They appear on flattened branchlets. It normally makes a large, dense, dome-shaped shrub, eventually to over 4m (13ft). Provides wonderful contrast to bold-shaped leaves. FOR, O.

## *Vitis coignetiae*
CLIMBER (DECIDUOUS) (JAPAN, KOREA)

A magnificent species of grape vine with large-lobed, rough-textured leaves that turn to crimson and scarlet in autumn. Try growing it up a tree – it will reach over 20m (66ft). You will hardly notice it during summer, but in autumn it provides a spectacular surprise. O.

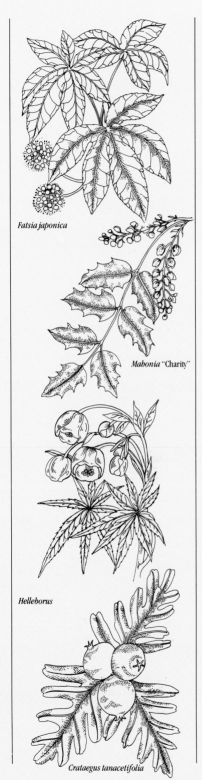

*Fatsia japonica*

*Mahonia* "Charity"

*Helleborus*

*Crataegus tanacetifolia*

# THE WATER GARDEN

*In any water garden you need a balance of aquatic (floating) oxygenating (giving air and life to the water) and marginal plants to decorate the pool sides. Here is a selection of some of the most useful in each category.*

*Nymphaea alba*

*Butomus umbellatus*

*Iris pseudacorus*

*Sagittaria sagittifolia*

*Alnus glutinosa*
**Common alder**
DECIDUOUS TREE (EUROPE, W. ASIA AND N. AFRICA)
A delightful British native reaching over 20m (66ft). Slender yellow catkins are produced in early spring, followed by coarse oval leaves. It is very tough, tolerating any site and soil. Excellent for the edges of a natural lake or larger pond. ALL, C.

*Astilbe*
PERENNIAL BOG PLANT
Astilbes are good value plants – hardy and thriving in boggy or just moist conditions. They cover the ground well, the flowers last long and they never require support. The flowers are borne in tapering panicles in shades of pink, crimson and white. *Astilbe × arendsii* is the group name for a long list of garden hybrids that grow up to 1.2m (4ft) tall. FLR, FOL, O.

*Butomus umbellatus*
**Flowering rush**
MARGINAL AQUATIC-PERENNIAL (EUROPE AND ASIA)
The pink, three-petalled flowers are borne in delicate umbels on metre-high stems. The narrow, smooth, rushlike leaves are bronze-purple when young, later turning rich green. FLR, FOL, W.

*Callitriche autumnalis*
**Water starwort**
OXYGENATING PLANT – SUBMERGED PERENNIAL (EUROPE)
This is one of the hardiest oxygenating plants. The long thin branching stems with small light-green leaves bunch at the surface in summer to form starry masses that are often eaten by fish. W.

*Caltha palustris*
**Marsh marigold or kingcup**
MARGINAL AQUATIC-PERENNIAL (NORTHERN TEMPERATE REGIONS)
A very popular water-garden plant owing mainly to its adaptability. It will thrive in dryish soil, mud or a few centimetres of water. The rich golden buttercup flowers are real harbingers of spring. The plants never grow taller than 30cm (12in) but can form quite large clumps. There is a white form ("Alba") and a double-flowered one ("Flore Pleno"). Always grow marsh marigolds in a position where they can be seen at a distance where they "shine like fire in swamps and hollows grey" according to Tennyson. FLR, O, W.

*Ceratophyllum demersum*
**Rigid hornwort**
OXYGENATING PLANT – SUBMERGED PERENNIAL (COSMOPOLITAN)
Another submerged, insignificant-looking oxygenator. The leaves are dark-green, rather stiff and forked. This species is exceptionally hardy and able to grow in very deep water (up to 10m – 33ft) and under very cold conditions. Remember that oxygenating plants such as the three mentioned here may not be attractive or even seen but they have a vital role to play in a living water-garden. W.

*Glyceria maxima* "Variegata"
**Sweet or manna grass**
MARGINAL AQUATIC-PERENNIAL GRASS
A beautiful waterside grass growing to 60cm (2ft) tall, with leaves regularly striped with green, yellow and white. In spring the new growth is suffused with rose-pink. An excellent foil for primulas but beware – it can be invasive and needs to be kept under control. FOL, O, W.

*Houttuynia cordata*
MARGINAL AQUATIC-PERENNIAL (CHINA, JAPAN)
An unusual, quick-spreading plant growing no higher than 25cm (10in). It will grow in flower borders as well as in bog gardens. The blue-green cordate leaves on reddish stems are joined in late summer by green cone-shaped spikes of flowers each with prominent white basal bracts. The leaves have a strong orange smell when bruised. There is a double-flowered form ("Plena") and, quite recently, much interest has been shown in "Chameleon", which has leaves variegated yellow, green, bronze and red. FLR, FOL, O.

*Iris pseudacorus*
**Yellow flag iris**
MARGINAL AQUATIC-PERENNIAL (EUROPE, ASIA MINOR)
Many species of iris will grow in or on the edges of water but the yellow flag iris is perhaps the best. The rich yellow flowers appear in late spring, on 90-cm (3-ft) stems above sword-like leaves. Varieties include "Bastardii" with soft yellow flowers and "Variegata", an excellent form with gold leaf variegations in spring. FLR, FOL, O, W.

*Lagarosiphon major*
**Curly water-thyme**
OXYGENATING PLANT – SUBMERGED PERENNIAL (AFRICA)
Often sold as *Elodea crispa*, this is one of the best oxygenators for all sizes of water-garden. It is a soft-stemmed plant clothed with brittle, narrow, curled leaves.
Like most oxygenating plants, it is normally sold in clumps clipped to a metal weight to keep it underwater. To plant it, all you do is throw it in the pool. W.

*Lysichiton americanus*
**North American skunk cabbage or bog arum**
PERENNIAL BOG PLANT (N. AMERICA)
Extraordinary, deep-yellow arum-like flowers appear in spring before the large (1.2m – 4ft long) paddle-shaped rich green leaves unfurl. It is an excellent weed smotherer, but the 30cm (12in) tall flowers give off an unpleasant odour, hence the common name. FLR, FOL, W.

*Menyanthes trifoliata*
**Bog bean**
MARGINAL AQUATIC-PERENNIAL (NORTHERN TEMPERATE REGIONS)
An aquatic capable of scrambling in and out of water and wet mud – excellent for hiding the often, all too obvious, edges of artificial pools. The thick bean-like leaves are trifoliate, the flowers appear in early spring on spikes, pink in bud opening to white, and fringed with long white hairs. Height 30cm (12in). FLR, FOL, W.

*Nymphaea*
DEEP-WATER PERENNIAL (EUROPE)
The water lily is the "Lady of the Lake", with its exotic, many-petalled flowers floating amongst emerald-green leaves. Loved by everyone from the Ancient Egyptians to Monet. There are 50 species of frost-hardy and tropical water-lilies growing all over the world. The flowers are delightfully symmetrical and often highly fragrant. There are many different coloured forms.

*N. alba,* European water lily, is a hardy, robust species with leaves over 30cm (12in) in diameter. The flowers can be over 10cm (4in) across. There are many named forms and hybrids available with a wide range of flower colours. This species is vigorous; for the smaller water-garden choose one of the many "pygmy" forms available. FLR, FOL.

*Osmunda regalis*
**Royal fern**
BOG FERN (COSMOPOLITAN)
The largest and most striking fern that is hardy in northern temperate regions. It will reach up to 1.5m (5ft) with its fronds that are pale green in spring, turning to russet in autumn. The separate fertile fronds that produce the spores look like green-brown flowers. Suitable for any type of soil that remains moist in summer. Looks good planted with yellow flag iris (*Iris pseudocorus*). FOL, O, W.

*Primula japonica*
**Primrose**
PERENNIAL BOG PLANT (JAPAN)
Many species of primrose will grow in boggy conditions. *Primula japonica,* sometimes called the "queen of primroses", is perhaps the showiest and most satisfactory species for a cool waterside position. Allow them to seed themselves about to give bold, random groupings.

There are various forms producing tier upon tier of brightly coloured flowers. "Miller's Crimson" is bright red, "Postford White" is pure white. To 60cm – 24in. FLR, W.

*Sagittaria sagittifolia*
**European arrowhead**
MARGINAL AQUATIC-PERENNIAL (EUROPE)
Handsome three-petalled white flowers with a large, purple spot appear in mid- to late-summer. The emergent leaves are arrow-shaped, the floating oval and the submerged kinds are linear. The flower spike reaches about 45cm (18in). "Flore Pleno", with double flowers, is very attractive and slower to spread. FLR, FOL, W.

*Salix alba* "Britzensis"
**Scarlet willow**
SHRUB OR TREE
A remarkable form of the white willow, conspicuous in winter when the branches are a brilliant orange-scarlet. Cut back hard every other year (like a dogwood) to get a mass of such stems. If not, it will make a tree over 10m (33ft) high. Loves moist conditions. W.

*Scrophularia aquatica* "Variegata"
**Variegated water figwort**
PERENNIAL BOG PLANT
The species is an undistinguished weed but the variegated form is superb – a striking evergreen with leaves striped and splashed with cream. It does best in semi-shade. Grows to 60cm (24in). FOL.

*Stratiotes aloides*
**Water soldier**
FLOATING AQUATIC – PERENNIAL (EUROPE)
Although a floater, this plant remains submerged except at flowering time when pineapple-like rosettes of spring leaves rise to the surface to reveal three-petalled white flowers from mid- to late-summer. This is also a useful oxygenator. FLR, W.

*Taxodium distichum*
**Swamp cypress**
DECIDUOUS CONIFER (SOUTHERN USA)
The most suitable big conifer for moist conditions. The fibrous reddish-brown bark, grassy-green filigree foliage that turns bronze-yellow in autumn, and overall conical habit make this one of the most attractive trees in any situation. When grown by water, large specimens produce peculiar knee-like growths from the root system which project above ground. This is the dominant tree in the Florida Everglades region and can reach over 30m (100ft). FOL.

*Ceratophyllum demersum*

*Primula japonica*

*Lysichiton americanus*

*Osmunda regalis*

173

# THE ALL-SEASONS GARDEN

*The plants listed below are definitely for the "all-seasons garden" in that they are all good value, providing decoration for either a long period through the year or have more than one ornamental attribute.*

*Prunus sargentii*

*Rosa rugosa*

### *Abelia* × *grandiflora*
SHRUB (DECIDUOUS)

The abelias are a small group of pretty, medium-sized shrubs that revel in full sun. *Abelia* × *grandiflora* is a hybrid and the most popular form available. The delicate pink and white flowers are set amongst small bronzy bracts and appear from mid-summer to early autumn. In mild winters much of the foliage is retained. To 2m (6ft 6in). FLR, FOL, C.

### *Amelanchier lamarckii*
**Snowy mespilus**
SMALL TREE OR LARGE SHRUB (DECIDUOUS) (N. AMERICA)

This is very much a plant for the all-seasons garden for it looks good almost all year round. In spring the young leaves are silky in texture and a warm coppery-red in colour. The flowers soon appear – white and in ample racemes. The small berries ripen to black by mid-summer. In autumn the foliage tints are red and orange (in the sun) and yellow (in the shade). This plant is very hardy, easy to grow and tolerates a wide range of soils, including almost boggy ground. Often sold under the name *A. canadensis*. To over 6m – 20ft. FLR, FOL, W, C, WA.

### *Arbutus unedo*
**Strawberry tree**
TREE OR SHRUB (EVERGREEN) (MEDITERRANEAN AND S. W. IRELAND)

A small tree or large shrub to around 3m (10ft) with deep brown shredded bark. The dark glossy green leaves are reason alone to grow this tree so the white, pitcher-shaped flowers and strawberry-like fruits that appear together in late autumn are a genuine bonus. FLR, FOL, C.

### *Aster* × *frikartii*
**Michaelmas daisy**
HERBACEOUS PERENNIAL

An early hybrid *Aster* between *A. amellus* and *A. thomsonii*. It is, by far, the best sort – very long flowering and much less prone to mildew attack. The clear lavender-blue flowers appear from mid-summer through to mid-autumn, and have a very special cool quality. It is available in two forms, "Mönch" and "Wander von Stäfa". FLR, C.

### *Berberis thunbergii* "Roseglow"
SHRUB (DECIDUOUS)

A very striking form of barberry, native of Japan. The leaves are purple, mottled silver-pink and bright rose. Compact in growth (seldom more than 1m – 3ft high) and unsurpassed in the brilliance of its autumn foliage and bright red berries. Another good all-rounder. FLR, FOL, O, C.

### *Buddleia davidii* "Harlequin"
**Butterfly bush**
SHRUB (DECIDUOUS)

There are many named forms of this shrub, which hails from China. It has naturalized all over Europe and will grow anywhere. "Harlequin" is a more compact form with reddish-purple flowers and creamy-white variegated leaves. The flowers are fragrant and very attractive to butterflies (hence the common name). This form will grow over 2m (6ft 6in), but all the *davidii* forms look better if cut back hard every spring. FLR, FOL, O, W, C.

### *Clematis tangutica*
CLIMBER (DECIDUOUS) (MONGOLIA TO N. W. CHINA)

This dense-growing climber (to 5m – 17ft) has deeply cut, blue-green foliage and strange rich-yellow, lantern-like flowers that hang down on delicate stalks in autumn. These are followed by silky seed-heads that stay on the plant during winter. FLR, FOL, O, C.

### *Cornus florida*
**Flowering dogwood**
LARGE SHRUB OR SMALL TREE (E. UNITED STATES)

This is one of the North American flowering dogwoods. Each flower has four conspicuous white petal-like bracts, in mid-spring. The autumn foliage tints are intoxicating. There are many forms and cultivars: "Cherokee Chief" has deep rose-red bracts. To 3 or 4m (10-13ft). FLR, FOL.

### *Euonymus alatus*
**Spindle bush**
SHRUB (DECIDUOUS) (CHINA, JAPAN)

A choice, under-used but readily available medium-sized shrub growing slowly to over 1.5m (5ft). It is distinguished by the unusual winged growths on all the branches which provide winter interest. In autumn the foliage reliably turns purple-red. FOL, O, C.

### *Hydrangea thunbergii* "Preziosa"
SHRUB (DECIDUOUS)

The hydrangeas are a very valuable group of garden plants and the mop-head or lacecap Hortensia types are extremely popular. Sadly, many of the other forms are less well known but are perhaps even more decorative. *H. thunbergii* (also known as *H. serrata*) comes from Japan and Korea. It is a charming dwarf shrub to 1.2m (4ft). The form "Preziosa" has purple-red tinged young foliage and beautiful globular heads of deep rose florets in summer. In colder weather the flowers and foliage turn deeper shades of red and purple. FLR, FOL, C

### *Lavatera thuringiaca* "Rosea"
(syn. *L. olbia* "Rosea")
**Shrubby mallow**
SUB-SHRUB (DECIDUOUS)

Very vigorous (to 2m – 6ft 6in) with greyish palmate leaves and large pink mallow flowers all summer. Does best in a warm sunny position. FLR, C.

*Mahonia* "Charity"
SHRUB (EVERGREEN)

This is one of the best mahonias from the media group of hybrids. The half-metre long leaves are made up of two lines of spiny leaflets. Fragrant, deep yellow flowers are produced in terminal clusters in long arching spikes throughout autumn and early winter. FLR, FOL, O, C.

*Parrotia persica*
**Persian ironwood**
TREE OR SHRUB (DECIDUOUS) (IRAN TO CAUCASUS)

A wide-spreading plant mainly grown for its red and gold autumn foliage tints. The flaking bark on mature specimens is most attractive. The flowers are sadly often missed, although if noticed they are quite surprising – just clusters of crimson stamens in early spring. It can reach over 5m (17ft) in height. FOL.

*Picea orientalis* "Aurea"
CONIFER (EVERGREEN)

A spectacular form of the oriental spruce from Asia Minor and the Caucasus. In spring, the new growth on every branch and twig is creamy-yellow, becoming darker and eventually green by the summer. To over 5m (17ft). FOL..

*Polygonum affine*
HERBACEOUS PERENNIAL (NEPAL)

A splendid ground-cover plant producing a carpet of simple leaves and a mass of 25cm (10in) high pink flower spikes that turn deep red with age. There are some good named forms; "Superbum" with superior vigour and colour is perhaps the best. FLR, C.

*Prunus sargentii*
**Ornamental cherry**
TREE (DECIDUOUS) (JAPAN AND KOREA)

A small broad-headed tree with pink single flowers (opening in mid-spring), framed by the bronze-red young foliage. The chestnut-brown stripy bark provides interest throughout the year. In addition, it is usually one of the first trees to show foliage colour of orange and crimson in autumn. FLR, FOL, O, C.

*Prunus subhirtella* "Autumnalis"
**Autumn cherry**
TREE (DECIDUOUS)

A small tree to 6m (20ft) that can flower any time between November and March. The flowers are semi-double and white. The parent species flowers in spring and there are other good forms including some with weeping habits. FLR, O, C.

*Rheum palmatum*
**Ornamental rhubarb**
HERBACEOUS PERENNIAL (CHINA)

The large palmate leaves of this rhubarb are very deeply cut and often tinged red. The crimson flower spikes appear in early summer and give the plant a stately height of nearly 2m (6ft or so). In autumn the foliage often turns russet-yellow before collapsing. Look out for the form "Atrosanguineum" which is more red in all its parts. FLR, FOL, O, C, WA.

*Romneya coulteri*
**Californian poppy**
HERBACEOUS PERENNIAL (S. W. CALIFORNIA)

A giant perennial to over 2m (6ft or so) with bold branching stems and deeply divided grey foliage. The huge white poppies appear from late summer to early autumn and have a central mass of dark yellow silky stamens. Needs full sun and good soil. FLR, FOL.

*Rubus cockburnianus*
**Ornamental bramble**
SHRUB (DECIDUOUS) (CHINA)

The mass of arching suckers are covered in a vivid white bloom and give a striking display throughout autumn and winter while the plant is leafless. The greyish, fern-like leaves are not unattractive. To 2m (6ft 6in). FOL.

*Rosa rugosa*
**Japanese rose**
SHRUB (DECIDUOUS) (N. E. ASIA)

This is a tough, thicket-forming species of rose to 1.5 to 2m (5 to 6ft) tall. The purple-rose, fragrant single flowers can be over 10cm (4in) across and are followed by bright red tomato-shaped hips. Its suckering growth makes it a useful,

decorative hedge or screen. In autumn the foliage tints are a fine butter-yellow. FLR, FOL, W, C.

*Spiraea japonica* "Gold flame"
SMALL SHRUB (DECIDUOUS)

The young foliage is a startling gold, turning softer yellow in summer. The crimson flowers are borne in flattened heads from mid-summer onwards. To get good foliage and a compact shape, clip over every spring. Never more than 80cm (2ft 6in) high. FLR, ALF.

*Stewartia pseudocamellia*
TREE OR SHRUB (DECIDUOUS) (JAPAN)

The stewartias are a small group of woody plants related to camellia. They require a semi-shaded site and a moist lime-free soil. *S. pseudocamellia* is probably the most readily available and the most valuable as well as being easy to grow. The simple white flowers with yellow anthers appear in mid- to late summer. The foliage shows up wonderful yellows and reds in autumn before falling. And finally the flaking scale-like bark is creamy-yellow, grey and silver-green. Makes over 4m (13ft) but is slow-growing. FLR, FOL, O.

*Stipa gigantea*
PERENNIAL GRASS (SPAIN)

This is a plant that you can't ignore. The blue-green, spear-like leaves strike out from the clumpy base like a static firework, reaching almost 2m (6ft or so). The huge heads of flowers are glistening purple at first, turning to soft yellow later. FLR, FOL, C.

*Viburnum opulus*
**Guelder rose**
SHRUB (DECIDUOUS) (EUROPE, N. AND W. ASIA, N. AFRICA)

A large, vigorous shrub (to 5m – 17ft) with maple-like leaves that provide attractive autumn tints. The whitish sprays of lacecap flowers appear in early summer followed by masses of bright red berries that stay on the bush well into winter. There is a gold-leaved form ("Aureum"), and one with large globular heads of sterile flowers ("Sterile"). FLR, W, C, WA.

*Polygonum affine*

*Buddleia davidii*

*Romneya coulteri*

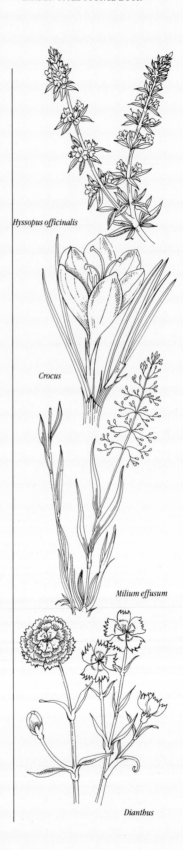

*Hyssopus officinalis*

*Crocus*

*Milium effusum*

*Dianthus*

# THE CITY GARDEN

*The plants mentioned below are all tough, good-value plants that are easy to grow and tolerant of atmospheric pollution. Many tolerate dark shady corners or open windy situations. For obvious reasons a number of climbers are included.*

## *Alchemilla mollis*
### Lady's mantle
HERBACEOUS PERENNIAL (ASIA MINOR)
The lady's mantle grows anywhere and is a good weed smotherer. The large rounded leaves and feathery sprays of small greeny-yellow flowers in summer are a delightful contrast to almost any other flower. (45cm – 18in). ALL, FOL, O, W, WA.

## *Cordyline australis*
### Cabbage tree
SHRUB OR TREE (EVERGREEN) (NEW ZEALAND)
A most distinctive plant with each branch or stem crowned by a large dense mass of long slender sword-like leaves. This plant, more than any other, will provide an exotic jungle texture to a city garden. Not suitable for very cold gardens. (Over 5m – 16ft.) ALL, FOL, ALF, FOR.

## *Cotinus coggygria*
### Smoke tree
SHRUB (DECIDUOUS) (C. AND S. EUROPE)
A tough shrub reaching up to 4m (13ft) in height. The round matt green leaves colour orange and red in autumn and the large plumes of minute flowers turn a smoky-grey in late summer (hence its common name). The various purple-leaved forms are also good value. FOL.

## *Crocus*
PERENNIAL BULB
Surely everyone knows and loves these ever popular dwarf bulbs (to 10cm – 4in) The gaudy, colour-forms of *C. vernus* are not my cup of tea. I much prefer *C. imperati* and *C. chrysanthus*, which are more delicate in shape, colour and size, and flower in winter rather than in spring. FLR.

## *Dianthus*
### Garden pinks
HERBACEOUS PERENNIAL
The genus *Dianthus* is a large and complicated one: it includes carnations, pinks and many hybrid groups. The garden pinks are one such group, producing fragrant, double-flowered forms such as the old favourite "Mrs Sinkins". The greyish foliage acts as a perfect foil. Normally less than 30cm (12in) tall, these dainty plants evoke the country garden for the city dweller and the flowers are excellent for cutting. FLR, ALF.

## *Hedera*
### Ivy
CLIMBER (EVERGREEN)
Ivies are tremendous city plants. There is no other self-clinging evergreen to match them. They grow in any soil or position. Allow them to climb up walls or fences or use them as dense ground cover under trees in dark shade or in full sun. *H. helix* is the common ivy and there are many attractive forms with variously shaped/coloured foliage. Also look out for Persian ivy (*H. colchica*) and Canary Island ivy (*H. canariensis*). (Over 5m – 17ft.) ALL, FOL, ALF, FOR, O, W.

## *Helichrysum petiolare*
SUB-SHRUB TREATED AS AN ANNUAL (AFRICA)
A wonderful sprawling, hanging plant with silver woolly leaves. The cultivar "Limelight" has yellow-green foliage, "Variegatum" has white variegated leaves. Very vigorous, excellent for tubs or hanging baskets, or as a summer filler. FOL, ALF.

## *Hosta*
### Plaintain lily or hosta
HERBACEOUS PERENNIAL
One could suggest hostas for virtually every garden style covered in this book. They are rightfully popular, thriving in sun or shade, dampness or drought. Mainly grown for their bold, normally rounded leaves of various tints, many species and varieties have attractive lily-like flower spikes that appear in summer. As a contrast to sword-like foliage or the filigree form of ferns they cannot be surpassed. Heights vary from a few centimetres to nearly a metre.

There are hundreds of species, forms and cultivars to choose from. My favourites include *H. sieboldiana* (very large bluish leaves), *H.* "Thomas Hogg" (clear cream margins to the leaves) and *H. lancifolia* (small, shining, pointed leaves). FLR, FOL, ALF, O, W, WA.

## *Hydrangea petiolaris*
### Climbing hydrangea
CLIMBER (DECIDUOUS) (JAPAN AND KOREA)
A strong-growing self-clinging climber easily reaching 20m (66ft). It is particularly good on a shady north-facing wall where it will still produce its corymbs of green and white lacecap-type flowers. FLR, FOL, O.

## *Hyssopus officinalis*
### Hyssop
PERENNIAL SUB-SHRUB (MEDITERRANEAN)
The leaves and young growth have a pleasant mint-like odour. It can be used to give strong flavour to broths, stews or salads. The gentian-blue flowers attract bees. Hyssop prefers a sunny position in dry soil. Ideal for containers. FLR, ALF, E.

*Impatiens sultanii*
**Busy Lizzie**
TENDER PERENNIAL – TREATED AS AN ANNUAL
(AFRICA)
The modern strains of bedding busy lizzies are great value. They flower from spring to autumn and grow well in deep shade – so often the environment of a city garden. There is a dazzling colour range. The "Super Elfin" and "Accent" strains are now well established. (To 30cm – 12in.)
FLR, ALF, FOR.

*Lonicera periclymenum*
**Honeysuckle**
CLIMBER (DECIDUOUS) (EUROPE AND N. AFRICA)
This is the common native woodbine of our hedgerows and woods. It is a vigorous twining or scrambling plant producing masses of sweetly fragrant multi-coloured flowers, from summer to autumn. The fragrance is especially noticeable on warm summer evenings. Normally available in the forms "Belgica", which flowers earlier and then again in autumn, and "Serotina" which flowers throughout summer and well into autumn. To 5m – 16ft. ALL, FLR, ALF, W.

*Matteuccia struthiopteris*
**Ostrich plume fern**
PERENNIAL FERN (NORTHERN HEMISPHERE)
This is a lovely, tough fern for the dark and moist city garden. The dainty fronds reach up to 1m (3ft) in height and are arranged in a definite shuttlecock shape – exquisite in their fresh spring greenery. FOL, O, W, WA.

*Melissa officinalis*
**Balm**
PERENNIAL HERB (CENTRAL S. EUROPE)
An erect branched perennial up to 90cm (3ft) tall with broad leaves with a lemon fragrance. White-yellow flowers appear from summer to autumn. It provides the lemon flavour for stuffings, fish and pot pourri and also makes an excellent tea. The variegated form, "Aurea", is especially decorative as a border plant or in tubs or window boxes. ALL, FOL, ALF, W, E.

*Mentha*
**Mint**
PERENNIAL HERB
A genus of over 40 species of aromatic plants widely distributed throughout the temperate regions of the world. A number of species and varieties are grown for culinary purposes, such as *M. piperita* (peppermint) for digestive peppermint tea, *M. pulegium* (pennyroyal), a shade-loving carpeter that is mint-scented and *M. spicata* (spearmint) for summer drinks and mint sauce. The form "Bowles Mint" is excellent for sauces, jelly and for flavouring new potatoes and peas. Most mints are quite rampant so contain them in pots or special beds. ALL, FOL, ALF, W, E, WA.

*Milium effusum* "Aureum"
**Bowles' golden grass**
PERENNIAL GRASS
This is a delightful form of a British native grass with yellow leaves, stems and flowers. I suggest it for the city garden because it is happiest in some shade and provides a marvellous foliage contrast for most of the year. To 60cm – 24in. ALL, FLR, O, W.

*Muscari*
**Grape hyacinth**
PERENNIAL BULB
A popular clump-forming bulb, producing spikes of mainly bluebell-like flowers in early spring. Never more than 30cm (12in) high. Ideal for tubs or window boxes. *M. armeniacum* and *M. tubergenianum* are the species usually offered. FLR, W.

*Pelargonium*
**Bedding geranium**
TENDER PERENNIAL OFTEN TREATED AS AN ANNUAL
A very large, highly decorative group of plants that includes the erroneously named bedding geraniums, often confused with the perennial, hardy cranesbills.

Pelargoniums are real "hobby plants" and many gardeners collect them like stamps or cigarette cards. The flowers are borne in rounded heads of white, pink, red or purple. Some varieties have attractive fancy leaves while the regal pelargonium has large frilled flowers and serrated leaves. Ivy leaf pelargoniums bear fleshy leaves on trailing stems – ideal for hanging baskets and window boxes.

You don't need green fingers to succeed with pelargoniums. They have few pests or diseases – all they need is plenty of light and a free-draining compost.

There are hundred of forms and varieties to choose from – all eminently suitable for even the smallest of city gardens. FLR, ALF, FOR.

*Pyracantha*
**Firethorn**
SHRUB (EVERGREEN)
Firethorns could generally be described as erect and thorny cotoneasters, to which they are very closely related. They are often grown against walls and will reach heights in excess of 4m (13ft). They tolerate being hard pruned or clipped. Masses of hawthorn-like flowers appear in early summer, followed by red, orange or yellow fruits in autumn. ALL, FOL, FOR.

*Rhus typhina*
**Stag's horn sumach**
DECIDUOUS SHRUB OR SMALL TREE (EASTERN N. AMERICA)
The large pinnate leaves turn a warm orange, yellow and red in autumn. Such large foliage also means that this plant is always sparsely branched which is a great advantage in a city garden. The plant is not overbearing nor does it cast too much shade. The form "Laciniata" has more attractive deeply-cut leaves. To 5m – 16ft. FOL.

*Sedum* "Autumn Joy"
**HERBACEOUS PERENNIAL**
This is an excellent autumn-flowering hybrid, ideal for brightening up a city garden at that time of year. The rich-pink flowers are produced in large flat heads, their colour fading through salmon to a warm coppery-red. The fleshy grey-green leaves are attractive all through summer. (To 60cm – 24in.) ALL, FLR, FOL, ALF, W.

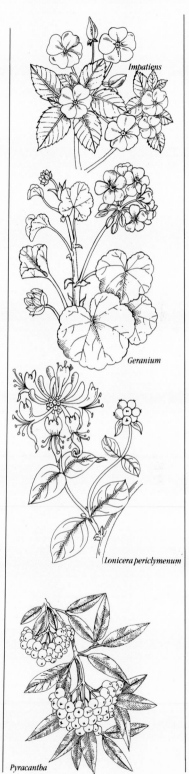

*Impatiens*

*Geranium*

*Lonicera periclymenum*

*Pyracantha*

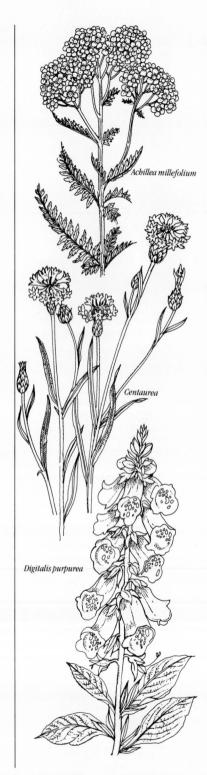

*Achillea millefolium*

*Centaurea*

*Digitalis purpurea*

# THE WILD GARDEN

*There are many types of wild garden, as this book shows. It can be designed in many a setting including woodland or meadow. The list of plants below tries to cover all these various situations. The plants come from all over the world but have in common a wild, natural appearance and feel about them. In many countries wild flowers are protected by laws. As a general rule don't pick or uproot anything from the wild; "wild flowers" are now commercially grown and available.*

*Achillea millefolium*
**Yarrow**
HERBACEOUS PERENNIAL (EUROPE)
Most of the achilleas have a "wild" feel about them, but this is the true native European form. The deeply cut leaves are downy and aromatic, the flower heads white (or pink) appearing from mid-summer to late autumn. It grows in grassy places to about 60cm (24in). Many of the cultivated yarrows have yellow flowers and are equally desirable in the wild garden. FLR, FOL, C.

*Anemone nemorosa*
**Wood anemone**
HERBACEOUS PERENNIAL (EUROPE)
A wild, woodland gem that is easy to grow in any shady border. It colonizes quickly in light or heavy soils and is a sheer delight in flower from early spring to mid-summer. As a wild plant it is usually white-flowered but many pink- and blue-coloured forms are available. Try establishing them in patchy, shady grass, alongside miniature daffodils. (To 20cm – 8in.) FLR.

*Aquilegia vulgaris*
**Common columbine**
HERBACEOUS PERENNIAL (EUROPE)
All the columbines lend themselves to the wild garden or border. This is the true common European species, so much loved by Miss Jekyll. The flowers can be violet, red, pink or plum in colour, and the foliage grey or green. It seeds itself everywhere and is easy to grow. FLR, FOL, C.

*Betula pendula*
**Common silver birch**
TREE (DECIDUOUS) (EUROPE AND ASIA MINOR)
A delicately branched tree hence the nickname "lady of the woods". It will grow to over 20m (66ft) in a woodland situation, but like all trees, tends to fill out and grow less tall in a more open environment. White bark, sharply cut diamond-shaped leaves and green catkins in spring. ALL.

*Buddleia davidii*
**Butterfly bush**
SHRUB (DECIDUOUS) (CHINA)
This shrub is a must for the wild garden as the long racemes of fragrant purple flowers are very attractive to butterflies. It grows to about 5m (17ft). There are many named forms, but for the wild garden choose a natural looking variety, such as *B.d. nanhoensis,* which has narrow leaves and mauve flowers. FLR, C.

*Campanula persicifolia*
**Peach-leaved bellflower**
HERBACEOUS PERENNIAL (EUROPE, N. AFRICA, ASIA)
The bellflower family is a large group of highly valuable garden perennials. *C. persicifolia* grows to just under 1m (3ft) and has nodding cup-shaped lilac-blue flowers that are excellent for cutting and which last all summer. There is a lovely white form; both can be raised from seed. Ideal for the wild garden, border or spinney. FLR, C.

*Centaurea dealbata*
**Perennial cornflower**
HERBACEOUS PERENNIAL (CAUCASUS)
The genus *Centaurea* is comprised of the knapweeds, star thistles and cornflowers. All are evocative of, and suitable for, the wild flower garden. The perennial cornflower grows to 1m (3ft) and is free-flowering and easy to grow. Each stem bears one or two lilac-pink flowers of great charm. The form "Steenbergii" has carmine-lilac flowers and is lower-growing. FLR.

*Cornus sanguinea*
**Common dogwood**
SHRUB (DECIDUOUS) (EUROPE)
Conspicuous in winter with its mass of ruby stems, it will reach nearly 4m (13ft) but can be pruned back like its American cousins. It produces white flowers from mid-spring to mid-summer followed by yellowish-white fruits. Plant it in bold clumps for maximum effect in the wild garden. C, WA.

*Digitalis purpurea*
**Common foxglove**
BIENNIAL (EUROPE)
The foxgloves are a delightful group of biennial and perennial plants. The biennials fortunately seed themselves around quite freely. *D. purpurea* has tall spikes of soft mauve-pink flowers and will thrive in a shady dell or woodland. The "Excelsior" hybrid form has spotted flowers. *D. grandiflora* is one of the perennial foxgloves and perhaps the best. It has soft-yellow flowers and grows to only 60cm (24in). FLR, FOL.

*Echium vulgare*
**Viper's bugloss**
HERBACEOUS PERENNIAL (EUROPE)
A wonderful plant for dry, bare and waste places. Generally hairy with pink flowers that turn to vivid blue with age. Related to borage *(Borago officinalis)* and alkanet *(Anchusa officinalis)*. All are valuable in the wild garden. To 80cm (2ft 6in). FLR.

*Endymion non-scriptus (*now *Hyacinthoides non-scripta)*
**Common bluebell**
PERENNIAL BULB (W. EUROPE)
Don't ask for this plant by its Latin name because it seems to change every year. It is normally available as dormant bulbs in the autumn – so don't collect from the wild. The common bluebell provides a spectacular display of natural ground cover to many of our woods in late spring. It prefers cool-shady conditions and is best planted *en masse.* The nodding stems of blue flowers (to 30cm – 12in tall) are unmistakable. There are also white and pink forms. FLR.

*Fritillaria meleagris*
**Snake's head fritillary**
PERENNIAL BULB (EUROPE)
The hanging, broad, bell-shaped flowers of this fritillary have a curious chequerboard pattern in pink and purple. It grows wild and seeds itself in damp meadows but tolerates quite dry soils and rough grass. Most colonies include albino forms. (To 30cm – 12in.) FLR, WA.

*Geranium pratense*
**Meadow cranesbill**
HERBACEOUS PERENNIAL (N. EUROPE, ASIA)
The deeply cut foliage turns to red in autumn and is reason alone for it to be grown in the wild garden. But the clear blue flowers in summer are equally worthwhile. There are a number of named selections – especially of double forms which seed themselves prolifically. To 60cm (24in). FLR.

*Leucanthemum vulgare*
**Ox-eye daisy**
HERBACEOUS PERENNIAL (EUROPE)
This is the big white daisy that grows wild in grassy areas. The flowers, with yellow centres, appear between spring and early autumn. Excellent for cutting. The "Shasta Daisy", *L. maximum* from the Pyrenees, gives a similar effect and is, perhaps, more readily available. (Both about 1m – 3ft.) FLR, C.

*Lonicera periclymenum*
**Honeysuckle**
CLIMBER (DECIDUOUS) (EUROPE AND N. AFRICA)
Our common native woodbine is a must for any wild garden. It will climb, scramble or trail in sun or shade, up tree trunks, amongst shrubs or perennials or over bare earth. The purple-yellow flowers appear in clusters from mid-summer to early autumn. (To 5m – 16ft.) FLR, ALF, C.

*Lythrum salicaria*
**Purple loosestrife**
HERBACEOUS PERENNIAL (N. TEMPERATE REGIONS)
Despite the common name the flowers are rich pink and appear in summer on slender spikes at the top of wiry stems. They will reach 1.2m (4ft) in any reasonably moist border and the foliage can produce strong tints in autumn. Look out for the few named cultivars that have been selected for their better flower colour. FLR.

*Papaver orientale*
**Oriental poppy**
HERBACEOUS PERENNIAL (ARMENIA)
A large group of wonderful flowering plants, a little apt to sprawl but which give a wild luxuriant feel to a garden or border. Heights vary from 30cm (12in) to well over 1m (3ft) in colours from orange or brilliant red to pink or even white. Their are many named forms that are easy to grow and readily available. FLR, C.

*Primula veris*
**Cowslip**
HERBACEOUS PERENNIAL (EUROPE)
A short hairy, delicate plant with deep yellow fragrant flowers. Growing in grassland, open scrub and woods – especially in alkaline soils. A wonderful sight in spring especially *en masse.* Plants and seed *are* available – don't collect your own! (To 25cm – 10in). FLR.

*Pulsatilla vulgaris*
**Pasque flower**
HERBACEOUS PERENNIAL (EUROPE)
Filigree foliage appears in early spring just before the cup-shaped nodding flowers that are normally mauve but may vary from pink to purple. It occurs wild in dry grass and on lime. The silky seed-heads last well into summer. (To 30cm – 12in.) FLR, FOL.

*Sambucus nigra*
**Common elder**
LARGE SHRUB OR SMALL TREE (DECIDUOUS) (EUROPE, N. AFRICA, W. ASIA)
To many gardeners this is a pernicious weed but it does have a place in the wild garden. The rugged bark, pinnate leaves and sweetly fragrant flowers in summer are followed by heavy, drooping bunches of purple elderberries. Both the flowers and the fruits are used for wine-making. This is a tough "grow-anywhere" plant that can be brutally cut back if it out-grows its position. It has given rise to a number of attractive cultivars such as "Aurea" with golden yellow leaves in spring and "Laciniata" with attractive fern-like leaves. To 8m (26ft). FLR, FOL, E, C, WA.

*Viola odorata*
**Sweet violet**
HERBACEOUS PERENNIAL (EUROPE)
A low creeping perennial that spreads by runners with delicate blue, violet white or even pink lilac or yellow flowers in spring and again in autumn. It grows wild in woods and hedgerows and a number of different selected forms are available. To 8cm – 3in. FLR.

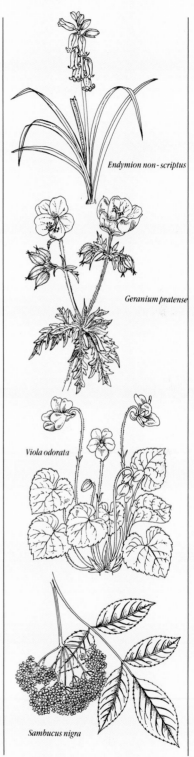

*Endymion non-scriptus*

*Geranium pratense*

*Viola odorata*

*Sambucus nigra*

179

*Laurus nobilis*

*Trachelospermum jasminoides*

*Rodgersia pinnata*

# AL FRESCO GARDEN

*For this style of garden I have tried to mention some high-class flower and foliage plants that can be enjoyed at close quarters. Other plants listed are aromatic or have highly fragrant flowers (especially in the evening).*

### *Aloysia triphylla* (syn. *Lippia citriodora*)
**Lemon scented verbena**
TENDER SHRUB OFTEN TREATED AS A
CONSERVATORY PLANT (CHILE)
A fascinating plant reaching, in the right conditions, over 2m (6ft). The flowers are pale purple and are produced in delicate downy terminal sprays. But the main reason for growing it is the delicate narrow leaves which give off a powerful scent of sherbert lemon! Protect in harsh winters.
FOL, C.

### *Camellia sasangua*
SHRUB (EVERGREEN) (JAPAN)
This is a noble *Camellia* species, sadly not often grown due to the fact that it is a little tender. But in milder districts or in a sheltered position, this is a most attractive winter- and early spring-flowering evergreen. The flowers are quite small but fragrant with a simple beauty that is most appealing. To 3m (10ft).
FLR, FOL, FOR, C.

### *Choisya ternata*
**Mexican orange blossom**
SHRUB (EVERGREEN) (MEXICO)
A pleasing evergreen with dark green, shiny trifoliate leaves that are aromatic, not unlike those of the Bay Laurel.
　　The white sweetly scented flowers appear in spring and early summer. A neat rounded bush, growing up to 2m (7ft), for sun or shade. ALL, FLR, FOL, FOR, C.

### *Clematis armandii*
CLIMBER (EVERGREEN) (CENTRAL AND W. CHINA)
An unusual clematis with dark green feathery leaves and in April/May large clusters of creamy-white flowers. This climber will reach up to 5m (17ft) and prefers a warm, sandy wall.
ALL, FLR, FOL, O, C.

### *Cytisus battandieri*
**Pineapple broom**
SHRUB (DECIDUOUS) (MOROCCO)
A lax shrub up to 4m (13ft) tall with grey silky leaves shaped like those of *Laburnum*. The flowers are in squat cone-shaped clusters, bright yellow and pineapple-scented. They appear in July. An excellent wall-shrub for the *al fresco* garden. FLR, FOL, C.

### *Daphne laureola*
**Spurge laurel**
SHRUB (EVERGREEN) (S. AND W. EUROPE)
Like most *Daphne* species the flowers are sweetly fragrant. They appear in February and March and are an attractive yellow-green in colour. The most attractive feature of this plant, however, is its simply shaped, leathery, almost succulent, polished green leaves.
　　A small shade-tolerant evergreen never more than 1m (3ft) tall. FLR, FOL, C.

### *Dierama pulcherrimum*
**Wand flower or Venus' fishing rod**
HERBACEOUS PERENNIAL (S. AFRICA)
Long sword-like leaves and arching stems of deep pink to lilac bell-shaped flowers that hang gracefully and hardly seem to be attached to the stems. Late summer flowering and growing up to 1-2m (3-6ft) once established. FLR, FOL, C.

### *Eucalyptus citriodora*
**Lemon scented gum**
SHRUB OR TREE (EVERGREEN) (AUSTRALIA)
Not completely hardy, but can sometimes grow to about 8m (26ft). Near a house, protected and well staked this is a fascinating addition to the al fresco garden. The foliage is large and glaucous and scented of lemon. FOL.

### *Galtonia candicans*
**Summer or Cape hyacinth**
HERBACEOUS BULB (SOUTH AFRICA)
A tall flower spike, up to 1-2m (3-6ft) long, of large, white, fragrant drooping bells appears in late summer. In a rich, well-drained soil it will seed itself freely.
FLR, C.

### *Geranium psilostemon*
HERBACEOUS PERENNIAL (ARMENIA)
This is a stunning cranesbill with deeply-cut broad leaves and in June, intense magenta-crimson flowers with black centres. Growing to over 1m (3ft), it acts as a wonderful contrast to orange flowers or can be framed and calmed by soft greys.
FLR, FOL, W, C.

### *Gypsophila paniculata*
HERBACEOUS PERENNIAL (E. EUROPE, SIBERIA)
This is florists' "Gyp" and there is nothing quite like a plant of *Gypsophila* in full flower – a rounded froth of tiny white stars over 1m (3ft) high and across. Grows best in full sun in well-drained soil. The form "Bristol Fairy" has pure white double flowers. FLR, C.

### *Hesperis matronalis*
**Dame's violet or sweet rocket**
HERBACEOUS PERENNIAL (S. EUROPE, SIBERIA)
Tall branching stems produce very fragrant white or lilac stock-like flowers in summer. A wonderfully simple plant able to seed itself, its scent is most pronounced in the evening. To 1m (3ft). FLR, W, C.

*Jasminum officinale*
**Common white jasmine**
CLIMBER (DECIDUOUS) (CAUCASUS, AFGHANISTAN TO CHINA)
This plant is a must for the *al fresco* garden. With its strong twining habit, it will reach over 6m (20ft) in a tree or will rapidly cover a pergola or arbour. The white flowers have a powerful sweet scent and last from June to September. It prefers some shelter in colder districts but otherwise it is easy to grow. The form "Affine" is superior with larger, pink-tinged flowers. FLR, C.

*Lathyrus latifolius*
**Perennial pea**
HERBACEOUS CLIMBER (EUROPE)
A much loved old-fashioned plant suitable for even the smallest of *al fresco* gardens. Train on sticks or trellis or allow to sprawl over a bank or patio, or over a shrub that has finished flowering. The pink pea-flowers are produced in late summer and early autumn. FLR, W, C.

*Laurus nobilis*
**Bay laurel**
SHRUB OR TREE (EVERGREEN) (MEDITERRANEAN)
Not only can this evergreen be used as a screen or windbreak, but it is also useful to have near the kitchen or barbeque area as the leaves are used in cooking. To 5m (17ft). FOL, FOR, E, C.

*Lilium regale*
**Lily**
HERBACEOUS BULB (S.W. CHINA)
Few people can dispute the beauty and the grace of lilies. The variation on flower type and colour gives the gardener an enormous choice. I have only room to mention one, although many are eminently suitable for the al fresco garden. One plant of *L. regale* will produce up to 25 powerfully fragrant, pure white flowers with yellow throats that are flushed with pinkish-purple on the outside. It can reach nearly 2m (6ft) and will grow in any good soil in sun or semi-shade. FLR, O, C.

*Lonicera* × *heckrottii*
**Honeysuckle**
CLIMBER (DECIDUOUS)
This hybrid honeysuckle has yellow-flushed purple flowers from July to September. It is said to be the most fragrant of all honeysuckles in the evening, therefore a must for the al fresco garden. To 3m (10ft). FLR, C.

*Lupinus arboreus*
**Yellow tree lupin**
SHRUB (SEMI-EVERGREEN) (CALIFORNIA)
Yes, this is a shrubby Lupin! Quickly growing up to 2m (6ft) tall with yellow, slightly scented flowers. Thrives in full sun and a well-drained position. Good foliage. FLR, FOL, W, C.

*Matthiolo bicornis*
**Night-scented stock**
HARDY ANNUAL (GREECE)
Just buy one packet of these seeds and sow in drills 1cm (½in) deep – you will be greatly rewarded. All through summer you will have a mass of purple or lilac flowers that open at night, when they give off a really powerful and much loved fragrance. A nostalgic annual growing to 30cm (1ft). FLR, W, C.

*Miscanthus sinensis*
**HERBACEOUS GRASS** (CHINA, JAPAN)
A clump-forming grass growing to 2m (6ft) with erect stems and gracefully arching leaves. It is often promoted as a quick-growing but interesting screen or hedge. There are some attractive forms such as "Zebrinus", the Tiger Grass, which has bands of yellow across the leaves in summer and pink-brown feathery flower spikes in October. FOL, O, C, WA.

*Nicotiana sylvestris*
**Tobacco plant**
TENDER PERENNIAL (ARGENTINA)
This is a tall tobacco plant growing to 1-2m (3-6ft) with huge candelabras of long, tubular white flowers with an intoxicating evening scent. Hardy in mild winters and freely seeding itself around. To 2m (6ft 6in). FLR, W, C.

*Pelargonium* (scented-leaved)
**Bedding geranium**
TENDER PERENNIAL OFTEN TREATED AS AN ANNUAL
A number of species and forms of this large group of popular plants have wonderfully scented leaves. Sadly they are much less known and used compared with their relations grown for flowers. Some of the aromas are quite extraordinary and create much interest in the al fresco garden. Try *P. tomentosum* which has large, hairy, pale green leaves and a peppermint scent, or *P. capitatum* which has oak-shaped leaves and a fruity-lemon aroma. "Prince of Orange" has stiff, serrated leaves and a delightful orange scent but is not easily available. To 30cm (12in). FLR, FOR, C.

*Rodgersia pinnata*
HERBACEOUS PERENNIAL (CHINA)
A bold-leaved perennial topped off in summer with imposing spikes of creamy-pink flowers. In flower the plant stands over 1m (3ft) tall and the large pinnate leaves, arranged in pairs, are wonderfully textured. Look out for the form "Superba" which is just that, with brilliant pink flowers and more lustre to the leaves. FLR, FOL, O, C, WA.

*Trachelospermum jasminoides*
CLIMBER (EVERGREEN) (CENTRAL AND S. CHINA)
A pretty climber with dark, polished evergreen leaves and very fragrant, jasmine-like, white flowers in July and August. It needs a warm, sheltered wall or could be considered for a conseervatory. Grows quite slowly to 2m (6ft) or more. FLR, FOL, O, C.

*Viola cornuta*
**Viola**
HERBACEOUS PERENNIAL (PYRENEES)
A clump-forming, ground-cover plant to 30cm (1ft). The deep violet miniature "pansies" appear in early summer and, if cut, again in late summer. There are some good forms including "Alba" (white) and "Lilacina" (cool blue). FLR, W, C.

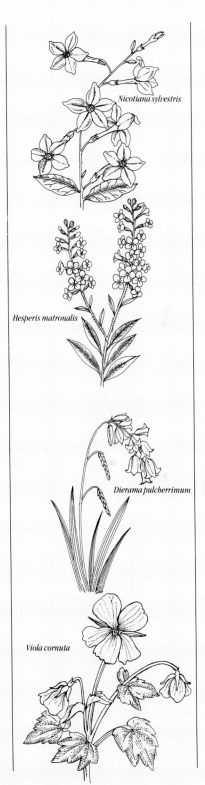
*Nicotiana sylvestris*
*Hesperis matronalis*
*Dierama pulcherrimum*
*Viola cornuta*

# THE EDIBLE GARDEN

*All sorts of plants are both edible and attractive, from vegetables and herbs to large trees. In the list below I have tried to cover the whole spectrum of plant types that are available for you to use in your "edible garden".*

*Beta vulgaris*

*Salvia officinalis*

*Morus nigra*

### Allium schoenoprasum
**Chive**
PERENNIAL HERB (N. HEMISPHERE)
Chive is an old and valued garden herb. The bright rosy-red flower heads give good effect in any border or as an edging in the edible garden. It grows to 25cm (10in). Look out for the form "Forescate" which has brighter and larger flower heads. Use in salads and soups. FLR, FOL, ALF, C.

### Angelica archangelica
**Angelica**
PERENNIAL HERB (SHORT-LIVED) (EUROPE)
A delightful herb, with large bright-green compound leaves growing to over 1.2m (4ft) in height. The large umbels of green-white flowers appear in late summer. A stately plant that will flavour stewed fruit, especially rhubarb. FOL, ALF, C.

### Beta vulgaris "Cicla"
**Swiss chard or sea kale**
BIENNIAL VEGETABLE
This lesser-known vegetable has never been out of cultivation since Greek and Roman times, but with the appearance of cultivated celery it has become less popular – mainly because it doesn't travel so well. Nevertheless Swiss chard is an excellent vegetable with a good flavour. It is easy to grow and produces more crop for the space when compared to spinach or spinach beet. Swiss chard has attractive pure-white leaf stems, and in ruby or rhubarb chard they are deep red. As with the decorative cabbages, they can be seen to great effect at Villandry, France. (To 60cm – 2ft.) FOL, FOR, C.

### Brassica oleracea
**Cabbage**
BIENNIAL VEGETABLE
The original wild cabbage is a native to southern Europe but like many vegetable plants the modern cabbage is a hybrid descended from the species after centuries of breeding and selection. The yellow flowers that appear in mid- or late summer are quite attractive but should not be allowed.

The reason why the humble cabbage is listed here is that there are some truly beautiful coloured leaf forms. Browse through any modern seedsman's catalogue and you will see these ornamental named varieties listed. Go to Villandry in the Loire Valley and you will see them used to great effect in the famous *potager.*

Treat them as edible bedding plants. They have fluted leaves coloured cream, pink and red. The colourful display lasts well into November. Height 30-45cm (12-18in). FOL, FOR, C.

### Cichorium endivia
**Endive**
ANNUAL VEGETABLE (ASIA)
A useful salad plant for autumn and winter use. Very popular on the continent. Its mildly bitter flavour can be ameliorated by blanching. There are many named forms but basically they all have a curly, cut mop of leaves that look most attractive in a decorative edible garden. FOL, O, C.

### Daucus carota
**Carrot**
BIENNIAL VEGETABLE – GROWN AS AN ANNUAL (EUROPE)
The carrot was known and grown by both the Romans and the Greeks but it was then

not eaten in Europe until the 14th century. It was introduced into Britain during the reign of Elizabeth I and later ladies of the court of Charles I used to wear the foliage as decoration. The delicate ferny leaves are indeed attractive, growing up to 25cm (10in) in length and the bright orange root is rich in vitamins. FOL, C.

### Ficus carica
**Common fig**
DECIDUOUS TREE OR SHRUB (W. ASIA)
A handsome plant for a warm sunny site. Large, dark-green lobed leaves and edible fruits. Look out for the named variety, "Brown Turkey", which is a reliable fruiter. FOL, ALF, C.

### Foeniculum vulgare
**Common fennel**
PERENNIAL HERB (EUROPE)
The common fragrant green-leaved fennel. The leaves are very finely divided, like hair. The flowers are like yellowish-green cow parsley. The plant can reach up to 1.8m (6ft) in height and the leaves and stalks flavour salads, fish and egg dishes. The giant bronze fennel (*Ferula* "Giant Bronze") is a more striking plant over 2m (6ft 6in) in height with deep purple-mahogany coloured foliage. FOL, C.

### Malus domestica
**Orchard apple**
DECIDUOUS TREE
A familiar tree, probably of hybrid origin. Apples are cultivated throughout the temperate regions of the world. There are said to be over a thousand cultivars – new selections are produced every year. A range of root stocks has been developed to give dwarf or semi-dwarf varieties. If pushed to recommend varieties, I would have to mention "Ashmeads Kernel"

(better than "Cox's Orange Pippin" and easier to grow), "James Grieve" (a dual-purpose apple, crisp and very juicy), and "Bramley Seedling" (the traditional cooking apple). C.

*Malus* "John Downie"
**Fruiting crab apple**
DECIDUOUS TREE
Probably the best fruiting crab apple. Flowers are white, followed by relatively large, conical, orange-red apples that are excellent for jams and jellies. An upright-growing small tree reaching over 8m (27ft) eventually. FLR, C.

*Morus nigra*
**Black mulberry**
DECIDUOUS TREE (W. ASIA)
Small but very long-lived with wide-spreading branches. Full of character, gnarled and picturesque, it makes a wonderful centre-piece to the edible garden. Fruits are dark red with much flavour. Seldom reaches more than 5m (16ft) in height. FOL, O, C.

*Origanum vulgare*
**Common or wild marjoram**
PERENNIAL HERB (EUROPE)
Another culinary, aromatic herb that is both useful and decorative. The mound of small dark leaves up to 45cm (18in) high is covered in small mauve flowers in summer. There are various golden-leaved forms. Use in bouquet garni, omelettes and stuffings. FLR, FOL, C.

*Phaseolus coccineus*
**Runner bean**
PERENNIAL VEGETABLE (GROWN AS AN ANNUAL) (S. AMERICA)
The runner bean was introduced to Britain in 1633, purely as a decorative climber for its masses of attractive red, white or salmon-coloured flowers in summer and green or purple pods until mid-autumn. It was not until about 100 years later that the runner bean was eaten.

Since they climb so quickly, they provide excellent summer cover for walls or fences, in the ornamental or edible garden. There are many named varieties,

look out for "White Achievement" which has good white flowers. Normally growing to over 2m (6ft 6in). FLR, C.

*Pyrus communis*
**Common or garden pear**
DECIDUOUS TREE
Like the apple, long cultivated and said to be a hybrid of multiple parentage. The blossom in mid-spring is particularly attractive and the glossy green foliage often gives rich autumn tints. "Conference" is self-fertile and keeps well, but for me "William Bon Chrétien" has the best flavour. FLR, FOL, C.

*Rheum*
**Rhubarb**
DESSERT VEGETABLE (PERENNIAL)
Although rhubarb is classified as a vegetable, it is eaten as a dessert. The large crinkled leaves and red sticks are bold and attractive. "Timperly Early" is the earliest and best all-round variety both for forcing and outdoor cultivation. FOL.

*Rosmarinus officinalis*
**Common rosemary**
EVERGREEN SHRUB (S. EUROPE, ASIA MINOR)
A dense evergreen up to 2m (6ft 6in) in height with grey-green linear leaves and clusters of blue flowers that appear in late spring. A traditional plant for the edible garden. Many named varieties. Use the leaves to flavour meat and jellies. ALL, FLR, FOL, ALF, FOR, C.

*Rubus idaeus*
**Raspberry**
PERENNIAL SOFT FRUIT
Raspberries will grow anywhere provided they are planted in well-drained soil. There are many named varieties including "Delight" (large fruits, heavy cropping), "Malling Admiral" (good all-rounder) and "Autumn Bliss" (good autumn-fruiting variety). W.

*Rubus* × *loganobaccus*
**Loganberry**
PERENNIAL SOFT FRUIT
A beautiful hybrid berry. The fruits are blunt, conical in shape, dull dark red in

colour and have quite a sharp flavour. They ripen from the middle of summer and the canes are only moderately vigorous. Choose the clone called "L.Y. 654" which is thornless. W.

*Salvia officinalis*
**Common sage**
PERENNIAL SUB-SHRUB (S. EUROPE)
The woolly and wrinkled leaves of the common sage are deceptively useful in garden design as a calming foil to more outrageous plants. The spikes of purple-blue flowers appear in mid-summer. Long grown as a sweet herb, there are a number of named forms including "Icterina" (gold variegation), "Purpurascens" (reddish-purple foliage) and "Tricolor" (white and pink variegation). No more than 30cm (12in) high usually. Use in stuffings, soufflés, pork dishes and with cream cheese. FLR, FOL, ALF, FOR, C.

*Santolina chamaecyparissus*
**Cotton lavender**
SEMI-EVERGREEN SUB-SHRUB (S. FRANCE)
A charming silver-leaved plant with bright lemon-yellow flower-heads. Not edible but makes a delightful dwarf hedge around a herb garden (to 45cm – 18in). FLR, FOL, FOR, C.

*Thymus* × *citriodorus*
**Lemon-scented thyme**
PERENNIAL HERB
A spreading bush to 30cm (12in), existing in numerous named forms, especially with golden foliage. Excellent with fish and poultry dishes. As the Latin name suggests, all forms of this hybrid are lemon-scented. FLR, FOL, ALF, C.

*Thymus vulgaris*
**Common or garden thyme**
PERENNIAL HERB (S. EUROPE)
Common thyme is used in bouquet garni, stuffings and with meat dishes. A spreading bush to 20cm (8in) with small hairy leaves and lilac flowers from mid- to late summer. There are many attractive cultivars. FOL, ALF, C.

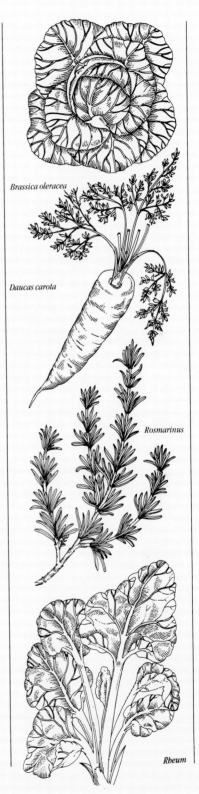

*Brassica oleracea*

*Daucas carota*

*Rosmarinus*

*Rheum*

# THE ORIENTAL GARDEN

*For a westernized oriental garden you need plants that have an*
*unmistakable Oriental feel but which thrive in the particular conditions*
*of your garden. The following is a selection of some native Oriental*
*plants and some others that produce appropriate effects.*

*Buxus sempervirens*

*Ginko biloba*

*Lysimachia nummularia*

*Iris kaempferi*

*Acer palmatum*
**Japanese maple**
SHRUB OR TREE (DECIDUOUS) (JAPAN)
This classic species is the parent of many forms and varieties. All have the basic hand-shaped leaves; many are deeply cut, some are purple or red in colour. All Japanese maples produce a wonderful mature habit and excellent autumn foliage tints. Some varieties are dwarf and weeping, others upright and quite vigorous. ALF, FOR, C.

*Buxus sempervirens*
**Common box**
SHRUB OR TREE (EVERGREEN) (EUROPE, N. AFRICA, W. ASIA)
The venerable box produces masses of small dark glossy leaves with pale young growths, and is indispensable in a number of different garden styles – including oriental. The shining, rounded leaves provide structural framework and restrained decoration. Will grow to over 8m (26ft) if left untouched. FOL, FOR, C.

*Camellia × williamsii*
**Camellia hybrid**
SHRUB (EVERGREEN)
Camellias are high-class evergreen shrubs and this hybrid (between *C. japonica* and *C. saluenensis*) has given rise to literally hundreds of different cultivated varieties. They flower from late autumn to spring in an infinite variety of colour, shape and size. Camellias prefer acid soil and a sheltered position. Fast thawing after a frost can cause the flower buds to drop, so plant them out of the morning sun. FLR, FOL, ALF, FOR, C.

*Chaenomeles × superba*
**Japonica or flowering quince**
SHRUB (DECIDUOUS)
One of the toughest and most easily grown shrubs. There are many named forms of this hybrid (*C. japonica × C. speciosa*), all grown for their joyful masses of flowers appearing in spring as the leaves are opening. Flower colours range from orange-red, through to crimson and pink. Can be free-standing, clipped into a flowering mound or wall-trained. Grows to 1.5m (4½ft). Try "Knaphill Scarlet" (orange-scarlet) or "Pink Lady" (clear rose-pink). FLR, FOR, E, C.

*Corylus avellana* "Contorta"
**Corkscrew hazel**
SHRUB (DECIDUOUS)
A curious variety of the common hazel with severely contorted and twisted branches that give the plant an oriental bonsai appearance. The foliage turns a good yellow in autumn and in winter the long hanging catkins make a striking picture. Also known as Harry Lauder's Walking Stick. It is slow growing, to about 3m (10ft). ALL, FLR, C.

*Cryptomeria japonica* "Elegans"
**Japanese cedar**
CONIFER (EVERGREEN)
A delightful form of Japanese cedar with soft feathery foliage that turns red-bronze in autumn and winter. Quite compact, making a plump column well over 4m (13ft) high. FOL, C.

*Enkianthus campanulatus*
SHRUB (DECIDUOUS) (JAPAN)
A distinctive shrub eventually growing to 3m (10ft), requiring an acid soil. The drooping cup-shaped flowers are yellow and bronzy-red, appearing in late spring in hanging clusters. Then in autumn the foliage tints are stunning reds, oranges and yellows. ALL, FLR, FOL.

*Ginkgo biloba*
**Maidenhair tree**
CONIFER-TYPE TREE (DECIDUOUS) (E. CHINA)
A remarkable tree with fan-shaped leaves that turn a clear yellow before falling. This tree is the sole survivor of a prehistoric family of trees, whose ancestors go back 150 million years. It is regarded as a sacred tree in the Far East and is often planted near Buddhist temples. Slow-growing but eventually makes a large tree of over 25m (82ft). FOL, FOR, C.

*Iris ensata* (syn. *I. kaempferi*)
HERBACEOUS PERENNIAL (JAPAN, E. ASIA)
The most beautiful of all irises. The rich red-purple flowers – that can vary towards lilac or white – are velvety in texture and the largest of all irises. There are many named varieties of different size and flower colour. Summer flowering, they grow to 1m (3ft) in height. FLR, FOL, W, WA.

*Kirengeshoma palmata*
HERBACEOUS PERENNIAL (JAPAN)
This is a delightful "one-off" thriving in deep moist lime-free soil. The leaves are broad and vine-like. In autumn cool-yellow "shuttlecock" flowers are produced in delicate sprays. There is nothing quite like it. FLR, FOL, WA.

*Ligustrum lucidum*
**Tree privet**
SHRUB OR TREE (EVERGREEN) (N. CHINA, KOREA, FORMOSA, JAPAN)
A handsome privet with pointed glossy leaves and fragrant white flower panicles in autumn. Can become a broad-spreading dome 7m (23ft) high or can be clipped for screening or for backcloth purposes. ALL, FLR, FOL, FOR, C.

*Lysimachia nummularia* "Aurea"
**Golden Creeping Jenny**
PERENNIAL GROUND-COVER (EVERGREEN)
A very valuable creeping foliage plant that gives an oriental feel to a border or bed. The small golden-yellow leaves tolerate a degree of shade and the single yellow flowers intensify the effect in summer. FOL, C, W.

*Nandina domestica*
**Sacred bamboo**
SHRUB (EVERGREEN) (INDIA, CHINA, JAPAN)
A truly remarkable plant related to *Berberis* but looking more like (as the common name suggests) an exotic bamboo. The upright, branchless stems are draped with large compound leaves, tinged red in spring and autumn. White flowers in terminal clusters appear in midsummer. Prefers sun and shelter. ALL, FOL, ALF, C.

*Paeonia delavayi* "Ludlowii"
**Tree paeony**
SHRUB (EVERGREEN) (TIBET)
Large, rich-yellow saucer-shaped flowers open in spring as the large, deeply cut leaves begin to unfurl. A bold shrub growing to 2m (6½ft) that will tolerate some shade. ALL, FLR, FOL, C.

*Pinus mugo*
**Mountain pine**
CONIFER (EVERGREEN) (MOUNTAINS OF CENTRAL EUROPE)
In Japan they use *P. densiflora* (Japanese red pine) and *P. parviflora* (Japanese white pine) to give that dense, dark, green texture so important for oriental-style gardens. In Europe, *Pinus mugo* grows better than these two species but fulfils the

same role. Very hardy, bushy habit, succeeding in all soils and sites. Dwarf forms are available; the species will grow to 3-4m (10-13ft). FOL, FOR.

*Prunus* "Tai-Haku"
**Great white cherry**
TREE (DECIDUOUS) (JAPAN)
The king of all Japanese flowering cherries, deserving a special position in a garden. Dazzling white, single flowers framed by rich copper-coloured young leaves in mid-spring. Makes a spreading tree up to 12m (40ft) high. FLR, C.

*Rhododendron (Azalea)*
**Evergreen hybrid azalea**
SHRUB (EVERGREEN)
Evergreen hybrid azaleas are often seen in traditional Japanese gardens, clipped hard into dense balls or mounds and flowering profusely in mid- to late spring. There are hundreds of hybrids and cultivars listed. Choose the "Kurume" azaleas in particular for an oriental look, such as "Hinomayo" (pink) or "Hinodegiri" (bright crimson). They will grow in full sun if the roots are kept moist but shelter and partial shade is a more natural environment for them. FLR, ALF, FOR

*Rhododendron yakushimanum*
**Rhododendron species**
SHRUB (EVERGREEN) (YAKUSHIMA ISLAND, JAPAN)
A compact dome-shaped *Rhododendron* reaching just over 1m (3ft) in height. The flowers are a rich apple-blossom pink that fades to white. The foliage is even more valuable than the flowers. It is leathery and rich glossy-green in colour; the new leaves in spring are covered in silvery down. Prefers acid soil. ALL, FLR, FOL, ALF, FOR.

*Salix matsudana* "Tortuosa"
**Contorted willow**
TREE (DECIDUOUS)
This is a contorted form of the Pekin willow. Vigorous, reaching over 10m (33ft) quite quickly, it has slender pointed leaves and green catkins that appear in spring. A graceful tree with an oriental feel about it. C, WA.

*Salix sachalinensis* "Sekka"
SHRUB (DECIDUOUS)
I make no apologies for mentioning another willow. This one is quite unique. If annually hard-pruned, it produces curiously flattened and recurved stems. Conspicuous, furry catkins appear on these antler-like stems in spring. Excellent for Japanese floral arrangements (Ikebana). WA.

*Sasa palmata*
BAMBOO (EVERGREEN) (JAPAN)
This bamboo is noted for its large, broad leaves – up to 35cm (14in) long and 10cm (4in) wide. It is rampant and forms a dense thicket. Not suitable for the small oriental-style garden – but provides excellent shelter and contrast where space permits. FOL, WA.

*Sinarundinaria nitida* (syn. *Arundinaria nitida*)
BAMBOO (EVERGREEN) (CHINA)
One of the most elegant bamboos, clump-forming with purple-flushed canes and delicate narrow leaves. An arching mass of stems up to 4m (13ft). Does best with a little shade and shelter. Often listed as *Arundinaria nitida*. FOL, W, C, WA.

*Trifolium repens*
**Clover**
HERBACEOUS PERENNIAL (EUROPE)
Common clover is a weed in lawns, but in an oriental-style garden it can be used as a creeping ground-cover and thus as a substitute for moss in a drier environment. There is an attractive purple form. To 15cm – 16in. FOL, C.

*Wisteria sinensis*
**Chinese wisteria**
CLIMBER (DECIDUOUS) (CHINA)
This majestic climber can grow to over 15m (50ft). The mauve or deep-lilac flower racemes exude a rich scent in early summer. The Japanese wisteria (*W. floribunda*) is just as beautiful. Both prefer a sunny aspect, on walls or pergolas. Alternatively, train them into a weeping standard. FLR, ALF.

*Pinus mugo*

*Rhododendron yakushimanum*

*Paeonia delavayi*

*Chaenomeles superba*

*Syringa*

*Aster novi-belgii*

*Clematis*

# THE FLOWER GARDEN

*There are over 250,000 species of flowering plants and we all have our favourites, so it is difficult to choose. Here are some of my preferred plants.*

*Aster novi-belgii* "Climax"
**Michaelmas daisy**
HERBACEOUS PERENNIAL (EUROPE & SIBERIA)
The species comes from the eastern United States and there are a large number of named varieties, both old and new. The cultivar "Climax" is an old one but probably still the best. It has good bold foliage up to 1.8m (about 6ft) and large wide spreading spikes of spode-blue single flowers. A magnificent perennial for the back of any flower border. C.

*Ceanothus impressus*
**Californian lilac**
SHRUB (EVERGREEN) (CALIFORNIA)
A large and varied family of shrubs from prostrate ground-cover to tall vigorous bushes or wall shrubs. Most have blue flowers – easily the best blue provided by shrubs in the northern hemisphere. All ceanothus require full sun and good drainage, some tolerate lime and many withstand coastal winds. *C. impressus is* impressive, although the name refers to the deeply impressed, small rounded leaves. The flowers are deep blue and appear in spring. They are so profuse on a mature plant that you cannot see any leaves – they are hidden by the flowers. To 4m–13ft. FOL, C.

*Clematis viticella*
CLIMBER (DECIDUOUS) (S. EUROPE)
Of this large group of famous climbers, I generally prefer the species or species types to the large-flowered hybrids. All clematis like their "heads" in the sun and their roots in cool shade, but having said that some of the hybrids pale in too much warmth and light, and are best planted in some shade.
*Clematis viticella* is a slender limber (to 4m-13ft). Their flowers are smallish in comparison to the many hybrid clematis and the petals narrow and delicate. The colours are, however, strong and distinctive.
Look out for "Abundance" with soft-purple flowers, delicately veined, and "Royal Velours" with velvety-purple, almost black, flowers. ALF, W, C.

*Daphne cneorum*
**Garland flower**
SHRUB (EVERGREEN) (C. & S. EUROPE)
The genus *Daphne* is a beautiful group of mostly fragrant shrubs that are small to medium in size. They all require what initially appears to be the impossible – a well-drained but moisture-retentive soil. This means that excess water must freely drain away, but the top soil must have a high percentage of organic matter and a good structure to be able to hold a reasonable amount of moisture and not dry out.
*Daphne cneorum* is smaller than most species but is a great favourite on account of its intense fragrance. The rose-pink flowers are borne in tight terminal clusters in late spring. It grows to just over 20cm (8in) but spreads further. ALF.

*Gentiana asclepiadea*
**Willow gentian**
HERBACEOUS PERENNIAL (EUROPE)
Most gentians are dwarf alpine plants with large blue, trumpet-shaped flowers, and prefer sun and lime-free soils. *Gentiana asclepiadea* is completely different. First of all it grows to 90cm (3ft) and has willow-like leaves (hence the common name). Secondly it prefers deep moist soi and a good degree of shade, and will grow even on chalk. The arching stems produce pairs of rich blue flowers that are unmistakably gentian-like. It is long-lived and reliable. FOL, WA.

*Hydrangea macrophylla* "Madame Emile Mouillère"
**Mop-headed hydrangea**
SHRUB (DECIDUOUS)
The mop-headed (Hortensia) hydrangeas are popular easy-to-grow shrubs, familiar to most gardeners. This is the best white cultivar – the florets are large with serrated sepals and a tinge of pink in the centre. (To 1 to 2m–3 to 6ft or so). ALF, FOR, C.

*Iris unguicularis (syn. I. stylosa)*
(HERBACEOUS PERENNIAL) (ALGERIA)
This is the winter-flowering iris. In fact, it produces its scented, rich lilac-lavender flowers, which are beautifully veined, anytime between autumn and spring.
It flowers better in a hot, poor soil, especially if it's ignored and neglected, and grows to 60cm (24in). The clone "Mary Barnard" is an improvement with larger, more readily produced flowers. FOL, C.

*Laburnum × watereri* "Vossii"
**Voss's laburnum**
TREE (DECIDUOUS)
Laburnums are small, highly decorative trees (to 8m-26ft) suitable for all types of soil. For trees they are relatively short-lived (30 to 40 years), but nevertheless still good value for the flower garden. Voss's laburnum is easily the best flowering form. It is a hybrid and inherits the best features of each parent (*L. alpinum × L. anagyroides*). It has the large densely held flowers of one and the extra-long drooping flowering racemes of the other. The bright-yellow pea flowers massed on a mature specimen in late spring/early summer produce a stunning effect. Laburnum seeds are poisonous, but this hybrid does not produce many. C.

*Lilium candidum*
**Madonna or white Lily**
HERBACEOUS BULB (S. E. EUROPE AND N. E. ASIA)
Lilies should be in every flower garden – they are perhaps the most desirable of all flowering bulbs. They have a reputation for being difficult to grow but this is a fallacy. For most species of hybrids good drainage and sun are the basic requirements.

The Madonna lily is no exception, so surround the bulb in coarse grit and plant in a warm border. The red-purple stem can reach up to 2m (6ft 6in). The funnel-shaped white flowers are very fragrant. Use Madonna lilies to make picturesque clumps in a herbaceous or mixed border in summer. FOL, O.

*Magnolia sieboldii*
SHRUB (DECIDUOUS) (JAPAN, KOREA)
All magnolias produce exquisite flowers but none more so than this species. It is a large, spreading shrub (to 5m–17ft) with glaucous leaves that are hairy beneath. The fantastic flowers are white and fragrant and appear from late spring to late summer. The most stunning effect is created by these delicate petals surrounding a central disk of numerous rosy-crimson stamens. O, C.

*Meconopsis betonicifolia*
**Himalayan blue poppy**
HERBACEOUS PERENNIAL (W.CHINA)
I can't resist listing this plant even though it has quite specific requirements – moist lime-free soil and a cool climate. The single poppy-like flowers are quite simply blue – blue as blue can be – with a central boss of yellow stamens. They appear in early summer, borne all the way up the stem. It is easily obtained and if you can supply the environment it needs, then it is a must for your flower garden. To 1m–3ft. O, W.

*Paeonia mlokosewitschii*
HERBACEOUS PERENNIAL (CAUCASUS)
A beautiful plant with a terrible name. Just ask for "Mollie-the-Witch", its affectionate nickname. Whatever you call it, it is well worth asking for! The cool lemon-coloured single flowers with long golden anthers appear in spring (earlier than most paeonies) above soft greyish foliage. It prefers sun and well-drained but retentive soil. Sadly it is not that easy to obtain. To 60cm–24in. FOL.

*Passiflora caerulea*
**Blue passion flower**
CLIMBER (DECIDUOUS OR SEMI-EVERGREEN) (S. BRAZIL)
The fascinating, slightly fragrant flowers can be as much as 10cm (4in) across. They are extremely complicated with many parts coloured white, pink, blue and purple that appear continuously throughout summer and into autumn until the first frosts. It is a vigorous climber producing a tangle of stems and a mass of not unattractive palmate leaves.

Hardy on a warm sunny wall where, in flower, it will be both a talking and focal point. To over 4m–13ft. FOL, ALF, C.

*Primula florindae*
HERBACEOUS PERENNIAL (TIBET)
This is one of the most beautiful summer flowers for moist or wet ground. It forms a handsome clump of large, rounded leaves from which several stems appear, bearing lemon-yellow, fragrant, bell-shaped flowers. A vigorous spreading plant to 60cm (2ft). W, WA.

*Prunus* "Ukon"
**Japanese flowering cherry**
TREE (DECIDUOUS)
Most of the flowering cherries are loud and garish in flower colour, but *P.* "Ukon" is a welcome change.

It is a tough, broad-spreading tree to over 6m (20ft) with semi-double flowers that are of the palest yellow-green. The flowers appear in April and initially are a stunning contrast to the bronzy young foliage. O, C.

*Syringa* × *josiflexa* "Bellicent"
**Hybrid lilac**
SHRUB (DECIDUOUS)
Everyone knows the many different named forms of *Syringa vulgaris* (common lilac). There is no doubt they are attractive in flower and scent but out of flower they are stripped of all their assets and lack any character. There are, however, a number of *other* members of the lilac family that are much more interesting and attractive.

The hybrid singled out here for mention is nothing like the common lilac. The slightly lax but massive panicles of clear rose-pink flowers are delicate and subtle. Each long, tubular flower has its own space and its beauty can be clearly appreciated. The fragrance is delicately sweet. The deep-green, ruby-tinged foliage is also attractive. Flowers appear in early summer. (To 3m–10ft). ALL, C.

*Tulipa sprengeri*
HERBACEOUS BULB (ASIA MINOR)
Most tulips, especially the many named hybrids and cultivars are best treated as bedding plants – lifted and stored after flowering. *T. sprengeri* is a true perennial and so does not need to be lifted annually. The small (for a tulip) flowers are a glowing deep orange-red and of a lovely narrow globular shape. (To 20cm–8in.) It prefers some shade and a damp but sandy soil. Plant the bulbs 15cm (7in) deep. C.

*Wisteria floribunda* "Multijuga"
**Japanese wisteria**
CLIMBER (DECIDUOUS)
Wisterias are perhaps the most majestic of all flowering climbers. Old specimens adorn whole sides of country cottages, or even stately mansions, with huge grey-barked trunks. The Japanese wisteria has slender, lilac-blue flower racemes which appear with the emerging pale-green pinnate leaves. The form "Multijuga" (often listed as "Macrobotrys") is magnificent with flowering racemes as long as 1m–3ft. The flowers are fragrant, lilac tinged with purple. It will grow over 9m (30ft). ALF, O.

*Lilium*

*Magnolia*

*Wisteria*

*Hydrangea*

# INDEX

Page numbers in *italic* refer to the illustrations.

# CREDITS

*All photographs by Ron Sutherland* with the exception of the following which were taken by:

Clive Boursnell 4/5, 30, 40L, 85, 87, 121
Brian Carter 4TL, 37, 38/9, 117L
Jeremy Cockayne 143, 162/3
Karin Craddock 77
Henk Dijkman 22L, 32L, 48L, 50, 54L&R, 55L&R, 60L&R, 81, 84R, 89, 102L, 103R, 149R, 156BR, 158, 158/9, 159, 165
Robert Estall 63R, 90R
Vaughan Fleming 28, 116L
John Glover 67
Carole Hellman 22R, 62/3, 145T, 156TL
Marijke Heuff 14L, 57L, 101R, 129R, 130, 131L&R, 132L, 135TR
Roger Hyam 53, 63C
Gill Marais 48R, 49L&R, 140, 140/1, 141T&B, 161
Marianne Majerus 3, 22/3, 88R, 90/1, 142L, 145B, 154
Anthony Paul 1, 14BR, 166
Jerry Pavia 27, 122, 138, 149L, 150
Brigitte Thomas 7, 8, 24/5, 26R, 33R, 52, 57C, 58L, 62L, 78, 80L, 99R, 110, 112, 113L&R, 114, 114/5, 115, 116R, 139, 142TR&BR, 146/7, 148, 152/3, 153R, 162L
Gary Rogers 18R, 120, 146R, 164L, 167B
John Riley 21, 26L, 160L, 187T
Alex Saunderson 84L
David Secombe 36L, 164R
Wolfram Stehling 105R
Didier Willery 146L
Jonathon Weaver 90L
Louis Wilkinson 56
Steven Wooster 17TL, 24R, 38C, 40/1, 60/1, 68L&R, 69, 86R, 132/3, 160R
Kate Zari 6, 11, 74/5, 100, 101

*Gardens and garden designers* are credited where information is available:
Michael Balston 72/3
Paul Bangay 157R
Miles Challis 46L
Murray Collins 70/1
Denman's Garden 10TL, 94BR, 136
Duane Paul Design Team 66TR, 70BL, 71TR, 76BL, 92, 118/9, 125BL, 126/7
Rick Eckersley 106/7
Paul Fleming 125R, 128BR, 128/9, 134/5
John Fowler 108/9
Albert Glucina 18BL, 107R
Brian Huxham 94TL
Frank Morgan 102/3
Pieter Plommin 33L, 45
Mien Ruys 20BR
Lisa Stafford 64
Paul Sheppard 4, 124TL, 135BR
Henk Weijers 46L
Peter Wydburd 92BL

Jacket photography
Front centre, top right, top left:
Ron Sutherland
Front bottom right: Wolfram Stehling
Front bottom left: Brigitte Thomas
Back: Brian Carter